"We must keep Christ at the center of all that we do,

in our own spiritual journey and

in the life of the church."

(Henry, 2022)

Historical Fiction by Susan McGeown:

A Garden Walled Around Trilogy:

- Call Me Bear
- Call Me Elle
- Call Me Survivor

Rosamund's Bower

No Darkness So Great

Windermere Plantation

Contemporary Fiction by Susan McGeown

Recipe for Disaster

Rules for Survival

The Butler Did It

A Well Behaved Woman's Life

Joining The Club

Embracing The Truth

The Keeper of Secrets

Nonfiction by Susan McGeown:

Biblical Women and Who They Hooked Up With

Biblical Warrior Women and Their Weapons

Jerusalem Times Magazines:

- Jesus of Nazareth
- The Twelve Apostles

C.S. Lewis & Me: Mere Christianity Told In Pictures

God's Phoenix Woman: Achieving The Triumphant Life

- Conference Booklet
- Inspirations

The Rise of the Mighty: A Study of ACTS

Believe & Obey: A Study of ROMANS

The Parables of Jesus

Old Testament 101

Colossians:

Walking in Wisdom

~What makes us different from all the rest?~

By Susan McGeown

Faith Inspired Books

www.susanmcgeown.com

Published by Faith Inspired Books

www.susanmcgeown.com

ISBN-10: 099031684X

ISBN-13: 978-0-9903168-4-8

Scripture verses quoted are from the author's personal favorite translation, the New Living Translation published by Tyndale House Publishers, Inc. 2008 Study Edition.

For additions, deletions, corrections, or clarifications please contact Susan McGeown at the above address.

Bibliographic and footnote credit appears at the end of this work.

This study is dedicated to:

North Branch Reformed Church

Bridgewater, NJ

www.nbrc.com

A place of love, fellowship, family, encouragement, learning, support, and endless prayer.

North Branch's Mission Statement:

"Overflowing with God's blessings, our hearts and hands reach out to the world."

Table of Contents

How To Use This Book

We are writing to God's holy people in the city of Colossae, who are faithful brothers and sisters in Christ. (1:2)

A church wide study of the book of Colossians! I hope you are all as excited about this adventure as I am. What fun it will be to spend the next few weeks study God's Word together as a family in both the Sunday worship services as well as our numerous small groups. May God reward our initiative with insight and wisdom.

Below is a "key" of sorts to the different parts of this book that you will encounter.

There are four main sections and they look like this.

Key Questions to answer look like this.

Key scripture verses appear like this.

(Numbers in parenthesis are scripture references in Colossians only.)

Definitions – words with definitions are bold and underlined on the page.

QUESTIONS: Questions that are appropriate for personal introspection or group discussion appear like this with space provided for answers and notes.

Additional information pertinent to the section appears like this in a text box on the right side of each page.

Interesting quotes from other authors appears in italics and centered here in this text box with bibliographic information in parenthesis.

WORD BANK: Wherever there is a "Fill In The Blank" or "Short Answer" activity word banks are provided.

PERSONAL THOUGHTS: Questions that pertain to your personal walk with Christ appear like this with a shaded box.

With the conclusion of each of the four chapters there will be two sections:

- **What are some of the mental images of the chapter?** – What mental images did Paul use in his writing to help us remember and understand what he was talking about?
- **How can I apply this to me and my church?** – Questions to help you apply these concepts to your personal life as well as your church.

PLEASE NOTE!!

Sue is ALWAYS eager and happy to receive corrections, suggestions, or insight regarding any of her books in particular her Bible study ones. PLEASE feel free to contact her and let her know your thoughts regarding this study: susanmcgeown@faithsinpiredbooks.com

Places of Colossians

Colossae – a city in the Roman province of Asia in what is now western Turkey, situated in the Lycus River Valley about 100 miles east of Ephesus. Colossae was a prosperous city as it was situated on one of the main Roman roads of the day. As a result, it was heavily influenced by many religions and philosophies of the day. (1:2)

Laodicea – a city in the fertile Lycus Valley in the Roman province of Phrygia, about 40 miles east of Ephesus and about ten miles west of Colossae. (4:13)

Ephesus – A large and important city of the west coast of Asia Minor where the apostle Paul founded a church. Situated at the mouth of the river Cayster, Ephesus was the most favorable seaport in the province of Asia and the most important trade center west of Tarsus.

Hierapolis – A city in the Roman province of Phrygia known for its warm springs and baths. (4:13)

The Apostle Paul never actually visited Colossae. He communicated through trusted messengers and letters.

Today, because of silting from the river, the ruins of the city Ephesus now lie in a swamp seven miles inland.

Today the ruins of Hierapolis show evidence of three churches, a theatre, a gymnasium, and many monuments.

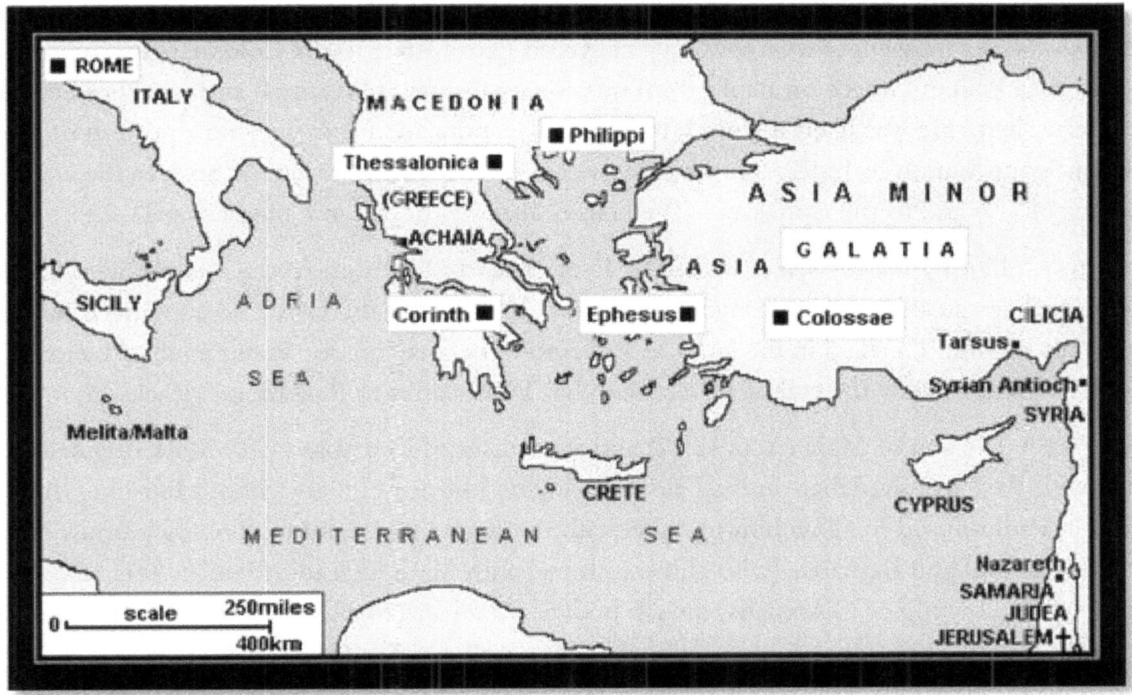

People of Colossians

Paul – The author of Colossians and approximately thirteen other books of the New Testament (some are disputed). Originally known as Saul of Tarsus, he was an apostle (although not one of the original twelve) and generally considered to be one of the most important figures of the Apostolic Age. As both an educated and influential Jew and a Roman citizen, he had significant advantage in his ministry to both Jewish and Roman audiences. His conversion is recorded in Acts 9:1-19. Paul wrote the book of Colossians (as well as Ephesians, Philemon, and Philippians) while in prison in Rome for teaching about Jesus Christ.

Timothy – (1:1) one of Paul's closest co-workers (he's also included in letters to II Corinthians, Philippians, I & II Thessalonians, and Philemon). Timothy traveled with Paul for much of Paul's missionary career. Timothy was commissioned by Paul to lead the Christian community in Ephesus.

Epaphras – (4:12) one of the first people to bring the Good News to Colossae. He was probably converted by Paul during Paul's three year ministry in Ephesus. He was "spiritually fathered" by Paul and visited Paul while he was in prison. He was a powerful instrument in spreading the gospel of Christ, having established the churches in Colossae (1:7), and perhaps Laodicea and Hierapolis as well. He was a voluntary prisoner with Paul so that he could minister to him as needed.

Tychicus – (4:7) a messenger who probably delivered Paul's letter to the Colossian church. He joined up with Paul in Greece on Paul's third missionary journey (Acts 20:4) and journeyed east with Paul to Jerusalem. He was likely a church messenger, responsible for conveying a portion of the benevolent contribution to Judea. He was Paul's emissary to transport letters, both to the Colossians (4:7-9) and to the Ephesians (Tychicus is also mentioned in Ephesians 6:21-22).

Onesimus – (4:9) A runaway slave (owned by Paul's friend Philemon) from Colossae who had fled to Rome, perhaps stealing money (Philemon 18). Paul led him to the Lord and convinced him to return to his master. Detailed in the letter to Philemon, there is "no document in all of history that has done more to remedy the evil of slavery than has Paul's letter to Philemon." (Jackson)

Mark – (4:10) The son of Mary (Acts 12:12) and the cousin of Barnabas (4:10) Mark originally traveled with Paul and Barnabas on their first missionary journey but left without finishing the trip. As a result, Paul refused to allow him to travel with them for the second missionary journey causing a rift between Paul and Barnabas (who chose to travel with Mark instead of Paul – Acts 15:39). By this point of the writing of Colossians, the rift between Paul and Mark had been repaired.

Aristarchus – (4:10) was a Jewish convert from Thessalonica (Acts 27:2) and at some point joined Paul on the apostle's third missionary journey (Acts 19:29, Acts 20:4) Paul called him a "fellow-prisoner" as he chose to voluntarily stay with Paul during his imprisonment in Rome.

Jesus/Justus – (4:11) a valued Jewish co-worker and a source of comfort for Paul. Nothing else is known about him.

Demas – (4:14) also mentioned in Philemon 24 and 2 Timothy 4:10, he is a coworker who later deserted. Paul wrote, "For Demas forsook me, having loved this present world, and went to Thessalonica."

Nympha – (4:14) woman who had worship services in her home.

Archippus – (4:17) coworker who is also mentioned in Philemon 1:2.

PERSONAL THOUGHTS: Who do you have?

Who are the important people in your life that influence you spiritually?

Who are some of the people in the past that have been a part of your spiritual journey?

Who are the people now that you consider to be fellow brothers and sisters in Christ?

What people do you wish to have in the future to help you continue to grow in knowledge and wisdom?

Life in Asia Minor During New Testament Times

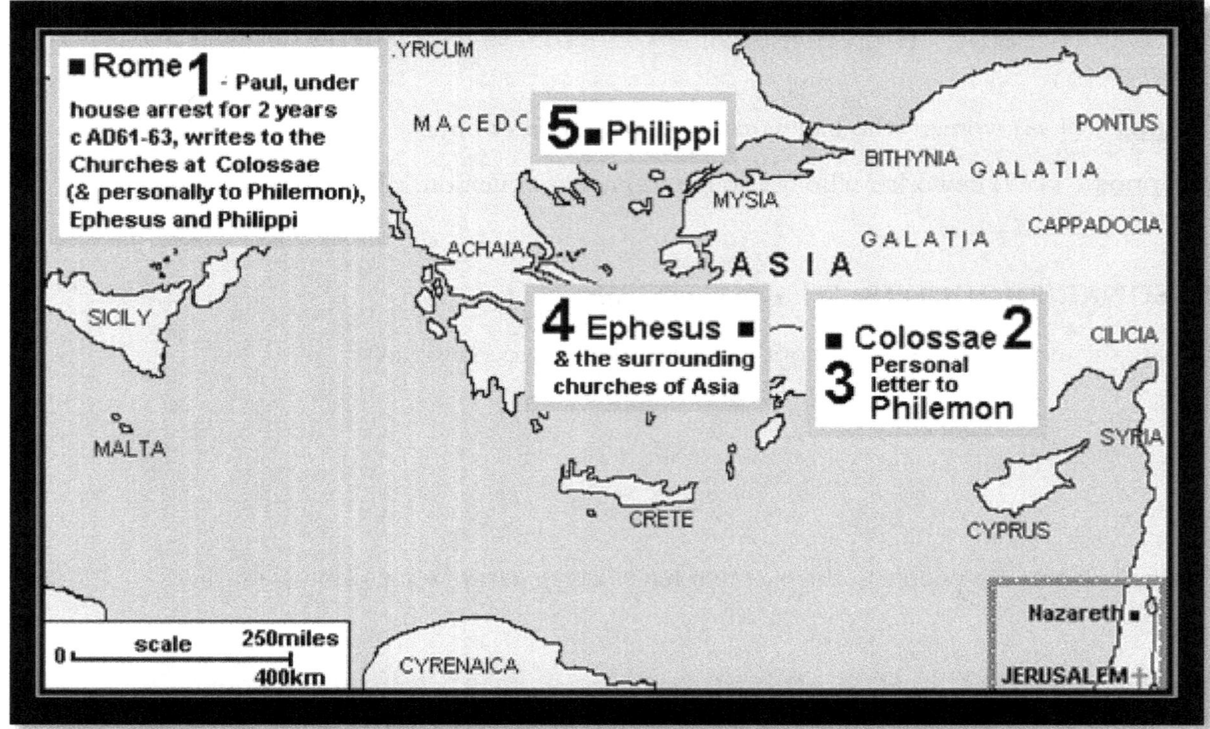

The Church of Colossae

- Composed mainly of Gentiles. (1:21)
- Founded by Ephaphras (1:7)
- Never visited by Paul.
- Philemon (recipient of the New Testament letter from Paul by the same name) was a citizen of Colossae and a leader of the church.

The City of Colossae

- Situated in the Roman kingdom of Phrygia, on the River Lycus, which is a tributary of the Maeander River.
- Was built on a major trade route through the Lycus River Valley
- Was a Roman province. The restructuring of the roman road system led to the city's demise.
- Located in what is now the southwest corner of modern day Turkey near the Turkish city of Khonai.

- Famous for the production of a dark red wool cloth called *colossinum.*
- The neighboring city of Laodicea was an aggressive competitor for trade business.
- Was part of a "triad" of cities in the area: Colossae, Laodicea, and Hierapolis. Colossae was destroyed by earthquake in 17 A.D. and again in 60 A.D. After each quake the city was rebuilt but never regained its early success. By the time of Paul's letter, Colossae was a small market town.
- By 400 A.D. the city no longer existed. It has never been excavated.

The Culture of the Times

- The Roman Empires was a dominant force in all aspects of society. The worship of the emperor as god dominated public life influencing the calendar, public affairs, and business ambitions.
- Besides the worship of the emperor, other pagan religions thrived. Romans were traditionally slow to violate existing sacred rights, preferring to allow coexistence as long as the proper hierarchy of authority was maintained. The worship of the god Men, the mother-goddess of nature Cybele, the fertility goddess Diana were prevalent all across Asia Minor.
- The New Testament period in Asia was the time of the *Pax Romana,* the Roman Peace. The entire area needed only local police to keep the peace with occasional Romans troops scattered throughout area hot spots such as Cappadocia and Anatolia. It was during this period that significant building of the Roman road system occurred.
- Roman Jews had the privilege of being exempted from emperor worship, military service, and some civic duties on the Sabbath and holy days. They were allowed to send temple tax to Jerusalem and practice their faith as the Mosaic Law and custom prescribed. It is estimated that of the thirteen million people living in Asia Minor, over one million were Jews. They were prosperous members of the community and engaged in virtually all occupations. Jewish boys were expected to follow in the fathers occupations and attended synagogue schools.
- Traditionally, families arranged marriages, and the father of the groom's family gave consent although the mother of the bride was also actively involved in the process. It is presumed that the bride and groom agreed. Marriages were specifically to preserve the economic and social position of the families and perhaps advance the career of the groom. Class distinction was adhered to everywhere throughout the Roman Empire.
- Roman citizenship was highly prized as it brought about significant rights and privileges. It could be bought at a very high price or was afforded at birth to children born to someone *who was already a Roman Citizen.* (Paul, in case you're wondering, was a Roman Citizen *by birth,* meaning his father must have been one as well.) (Acts 22:27)

- Mothers had heavy influence on children in all areas in the early years. Fathers coached their sons to follow in their career, however, within the first century there were more options available than ever before for young people. Education was emphasized and boys were often educated well into their late teens and early twenties. Information regarding education for girls is sketchy at best.
- Occupations were many and varied with textile production the most important industry throughout Asia Minor. Herders of sheep (necessary for the wool they produced), woolen goods makers (cloth, tapestries, blankets, curtains, fine rain repellant cloaks, tunics,), dyers (red, purple, glossy black), and wool washers, fullers, dyers, spinners, and weavers were popular jobs. In addition, specific cities also specialized in other fabrics such as linen, cotton, and silk. Other professions included tanners, bakers, parchment makers, builders, iron work, gold- and silversmiths, potters, and shipbuilding.
- Travel and commerce were heavily influenced by weather. Travel by sea was preferred over travel by land which was difficult. From November 10 to March 10 the Mediterranean was effectively closed due frequent to dangerous storms. Much of the trade remained local and Asia Minor required little in imports. The Romans built and maintained roads all over the province.

PERSONAL THOUGHTS: What is the culture of your time?

What aspects of society today hinders the spread of Christ's message?

What aspects of life interfere with active, regular participation in church? Bible study? Prayer?

Chapter 1: WALKING WITH JESUS

And by this we know that we have come to know him, if we keep his commandments. Whoever says "I know him" but does not keep his commandments is a liar, and the truth is not in him, but whoever keeps his word, in him truly the love of God is perfected. By this we may know that we are in him: whoever says he abides in him ought to walk in the same way in which he walked. I John 2:3-6

Questions to consider as you read and study this first chapter of Colossians:

1. What are the Good News facts?
2. What are things worth praying for?
3. Who is the Person of Jesus Christ?
4. What does reconciliation really mean?
5. What is the Good News secret?
6. Who is this guy Paul?
7. What are the mental images of Colossians 1?
8. How does this apply to me and my church?

What are the Good News facts?

Colossians 1:1-8

We have heard of your faith in Christ Jesus. (1:4)

The term "**gospel**" actually means "good news." So the Gospel of Jesus Christ is the **Good News** of Jesus Christ! Jesus Christ has solved the problem of sin through His death, burial, and resurrection.

In Colossians 1:1-8, Paul discusses the Good News of Jesus Christ. Use the word bank (and the scripture references) to help you fill in the blanks below.

1. The Good News centers solely on the person of ____________________. (1:4)
2. The Good News involves ____________________ in Jesus Christ, ____________________ for all God's people, and ____________________ of what God has reserved for believers in heaven. (1:4-5)
3. The Good News is the word of ____________________. (1:5)
4. The Good News is for the whole ____________________. (1:6a)
5. The Good News bears ____________________ everywhere by changing lives. (1:6b
6. The Good News is a message of God's ____________________. (1:6c)

WORD BANK: faith, Jesus Christ, hope, fruit, truth, grace, world, love,

Saving Faith – a commitment to Jesus Christ involving mind, body, and will. (Matthew 22:37)

"Faith – Love – Hope – we must never be satisfied unless we see in ourselves and our fellow Christians these three delightful fruits of the Spirit."
(Spurgeon, Loc 21)

"Faith lifts us above the world.
Love preserves us from selfishness.
Hope keeps us up under trials."
(Spurgeon, Loc 23)

"Faith hears God's Word.
Love is evidence of true salvation.
Hope is the characteristic of a believer."
(Wiersbe, 27-28)

"God's People" – (1:4) literally *holy ones* or *saints.* Through Jesus Christ's sacrifice on the cross, all believers are declared holy (perfect) in God's eyes. (See 3:12)

What things are worth praying for?

Colossians 1:9-14

"So we have not stopped praying for you since we first heard about you." (1:9)

Prayer is ______________________. How do you fill in this blank? Since I've already written a whole book about prayer it's particularly hard to come up with a short response. I like how Matt Slick explained it: *Prayer is the privilege of touching the heart of the Father through the Son of God, Jesus our Lord.*

Paul, knowing the critical importance of prayer and recognizing that many of us have concerns about whether or not we 'get it right' regularly wrote specifically about what he prayed about. His list in Colossians 1:9-14 is a concise guide for believers everywhere of the things worth praying for.

Pray for the Believer's Wisdom (3:9-10b)

- **Learn** - To gain knowledge through study, instruction and experience.
- **Knowledge** – facts or the ability to grasp the truth.
- **Understanding** - comprehension of facts or to "place together", the ability to assess things.
- **Wisdom**: Using both our knowledge and understanding of God's Will to have a successful Christian life or the ability to defend what we understand.

QUESTION: What is God's Will for all believers?
(Romans 12:2, I Thess. 5:16-19, John 14:15; Proverbs 3:5-6, Matthew 28:16-20)

"When a person is born into God's family by faith in Jesus Christ, he is born with all that he needs for growth and maturity." (Wiersbe, 33)

"The Will of God is an important part of a successful Christian life. God wants us to know His Will (Acts 22:14) and understand it. (Ephesians 5:17)" (Wiersbe, 34)

"We understand the Will of God through the Word of God." (Wiersbe, 34)

"What a valuable thing it is to know and understand the Will of God! (Spurgeon, Loc42)

Pray for the Believer's Goal (1:10a)

- **Please** – to give satisfaction, be agreeable
- **Honor** – high respect, recognition, esteem

QUESTION: What are the Fruits of the Spirit? Galatians 5:22-23

Pray for the Believer's Energy (1:11)

- **Endurance** – perseverance, the ability to keep on going despite hardships
- **Patience** – calm, tolerant, even-tempered behavior in the face of diversity and hardships

QUESTION: Sin is humanity's greatest problem. How is a believer impacted by this fact?

Spiritual intelligence is the beginning of a successful, fruitful Christian life. (Wiersbe, 35)

"We do not know the grace of God in truth unless it brings for fruit in us." (Spurgeon Loc 26)

Patience is endurance when *things* are difficult. **Long-suffering** is self-restraint when *people* are difficult.

Pray for the Believer's Attitude (1:11b-12)

- **Joy** – great pleasure independent of circumstances or people (which is different from happiness which is dependent on circumstances or people)
- **Thanksgiving** – aware and appreciative of a benefit, grateful

QUESTION: What do believers have to be thankful for? (1:13-14)

PERSONAL THOUGHTS: What good are you to God?

Can you articulate what God's Will is for you?

What are your spiritual fruits? How do you shine?

What areas in life are your greatest struggles? How do you cope?

What blessings has God given you to empower you?

"Knowledge, conduct, service and character must always go together." (Wiersbe, 39)

"Thankfulness is the opposite of selfishness." (Wiersb22e, 42)

Who is the Person of Jesus Christ?

Colossians 1:15-20

Christ is the visible image of the invisible God. 1:15

Creeds are statements of belief. The Latin word *credo* means simply "I believe." Prior to the written word and the ready availability of Bibles, creeds were the key to spreading factual information in an accurate and succinct manner. They were necessary to clarify the Christian faith and distinguish true content from error and false representations of the faith. They were not intended to be comprehensive but to be a summary of core beliefs. The creed (or possibly a hymn) listed in Colossians 1:15-20 regarding the supremacy of Christ is one of the earliest, dated around A.D. 60-62.

Let's look more closely at exactly what Paul is claiming about the Person of Jesus Christ.

Jesus Christ is visible God on earth. (1:15-17)

Interesting things about these verses:

- The Greek word that Paul uses to describe Jesus in 1:15 is ***eikon*** which means "Image, representation" and is used to refer to human beings having been made in the image of God. (Strong, #1504) See Genesis 1:26-27
- Jesus is referred to as 'firstborn' not to imply that he was created but in reference to his supremacy of rank and priority as spoken of in the Old Testament. See Psalm 89:27.
- "Thrones, kingdoms, rulers, and authorities in the unseen world" - Paul made an effort to cover all bases regarding powers both seen and unseen in the world. This isn't the only time Paul refers to things in the "unseen world". See Ephesians 6:13

Other early New Testament creeds include:
*I Corinthians 15:3-7 (AD 54-55) The Resurrection of Christ
*Philippians 2:6-11 (AD 60-62) Have the Attitude of Christ
*I Timothy 2:5-6 (AD 62-64)
*I Timothy 3:16 (AD 62-64)
*Romans 10:9-10 (AD 57)
*I Corinthians 8:6 (AD 55

Eikon is also used to describe Wisdom in the book of Wisdom 7:25-26 ("Wisdom is the warm breath of God's power. She pours forth from the all-powerful one's pure glory. Therefore, nothing impure can enter her. She's the brightness that shines forth from eternal light. She's a mirror that flawlessly reflects God's activity. She's the perfect image of God's goodness.") The theme of wisdom regarding Jesus Christ also appears in I Corinthians 1:24, and 30.

- "Created through Him" – Just in case you haven't gotten the entire picture: Jesus Christ was the one through whom all things were created and the goal of all creation.

"Jesus Christ is the reason for creation and the goal of creation."
(NLT, note 1:16)

"Christ is not so much what *we preach as* whom *we preach."*
(Spurgeon, Loc 94)

QUESTION: What words and phrases does Paul use to help us understand that Jesus and God are equal?

Jesus Christ is the Head of the church. (1:18-20)

The Greek word that Paul uses to describe Jesus in 1:18 is ***kephale*** which means "head" and usually has the meaning of *authority over* or *chief*. (Strong, #2776) (This isn't the only time Paul makes reference to this. See 2:10, Ephesians 4:15, 5:23)

QUESTION: When Paul uses the word "church," to what is he specifically referring to?

Jesus Christ is the fullness of God on earth. (1:19)

This isn't just Paul's interpretation of things! Jesus himself claimed this in John 14:6-7: *"I am the way, the truth, and the life. No one can come to the Father except through me. If you had really known me, you would know who my Father is. From now on, you do know him and have seen him!"*

QUESTION: What is the definition of fullness?

PERSONAL THOUGHTS: What is your relationship with Jesus Christ like?

Can you articulate what Jesus Christ means to you?

Can others see Jesus Christ's influence in your life?

How do you understand the concept of the Trinity?

What does Reconciliation really mean?

Colossians 1:21-23

Through Jesus Christ God reconciled everything to himself. (1:20)

Reconcile means to reestablish a close relationship between distant things. Paul describes the state of humanity in Colossians 1:21:

- We are God's enemy.
- We are separated, far away from God.
- We have evil thoughts and do evil actions.

God cannot be in the presence of sin. **Sin** – a condition of estrangement from God resulting from disobedience to the known will of God causes us to be God's enemy, fully separated from Him. And there is nothing we can to fix it. The entire Old Testament chronicles the attempt for humanity to return to the perfect relationship with God that Adam and Eve enjoyed in the garden before the fall. With no success.

This is the reason for Christ's death and resurrection. The need for us to become reconciled. Paul talked about this in Romans 5:10 *For since our friendship with God was restored by the death of his Son while we were still his enemies, we will certainly be saved through the life of his Son.* And in II Corinthians 5:18-19, too: *"And all of this is a gift from God, who brought us back to himself through Christ. And God has given us this task of reconciling people to him. For God was in Christ, reconciling the world to himself, no longer counting people's sins against them. And he gave us this wonderful message of reconciliation. So we are Christ's ambassadors; God is making his appeal through us. We speak for Christ when we plead, "Come back to God!" For God made Christ, who never sinned, to be the offering for our sin, so that we could be made right with God through Christ."*

"There will never be any mighty work come from *us unless there is first a mighty work* in *us." (Spurgeon, Loc 99)*

"Nothing can come out of a man but what God puts into him." (Spurgeon, Loc 99)

GOD, Sin ... & Us

GOD: LIGHT

God is light, and there is no darkness in Him at all. I John 1:5

Light and darkness cannot coexist together. You either have one or the other.

God and sin are like that.

Sin in our lives makes us incapable of being in God's presence.

Our choice is to live without God or find a remedy to our sin.

Sin: Darkness

People loved the darkness more than the light, for their actions were evil. John 3:19

QUESTION: How would you describe the current state of humanity? (1:21)

With the Good News of Jesus Christ, a new opportunity is offered to humanity.

- To be a part of the death of Christ. (1:22)
- To be one in the presence of Jesus Christ (1:22)
- To be **holy** – pure, sinless, perfect, blameless (1:22)

QUESTION: What do we gain through Jesus Christ's reconciliation? (1:22)

As believers we must:

1. ______________________________ in the truth. (1:23)
2. ______________________________ in the truth. (1:23)
3. Don't ______________________________ from the truth. (1:23)

WORD BANK: drift away, believe, stand firm

QUESTION: What is the Truth? (John 14:6)

PERSONAL THOUGHTS: What is my understanding of all this?

Can you articulate exactly how sin affects our relationship with God?

What does reconciliation mean to you?

In your own words, what is the truth of Jesus Christ?

What is the Good News secret?

Colossians 1:24-29

This message was kept **secret** *for centuries and generations past, but now it has been revealed to God's people. Colossians 1:26*

God's plan has always existed. It's been mapped out through all of history but has been hidden from human eyes. With God's decision to reveal much of His plan, humanity has now been 'let in on the secret'. The full scope of the secret has not been revealed however. Read the following list of events. Which have already been revealed? Which are we still waiting to see?

_____1. The secret regarding the salvation of Israel. (Romans 11:25)
_____2. The secret that Gentiles as well as Jews will be fellow heirs to God's promise. (Ephesians 3:1-9, Romans 16:25, Colossians 1:27)
_____3. The secret regarding the transformation of believers. (I Corinthians 15:51)
_____4. The secret regarding the fact that all believers will be indwelt by Christ. (Colossians 1:27, 2:2)
_____5. The secret regarding the union of Christ and the church is like husband and wife. (Ephesians 5:32)
_____6. The secret regarding the time of Christ's return. (I Thessalonians 5:1-4)
_____7. The secret regarding the coming of the Messiah and how He would be revealed to us. (I Timothy 3:16)

Answers: Revealed: 2, 3, 4, 5, 7 Not Revealed Yet: 1, 6.

Colossians isn't the only time Paul refers to the secret – the mystery – of the Good News. Check out I Corinthians 2:1, 7, 10, 13:2, 15:51, Ephesians 3:9, and I Timothy 3:9.

"The treasures of wisdom are hid not from us but for us in Christ." (Henry, 1435)

In Him lie hidden all the treasures of wisdom and knowledge. 2:3

Who was this guy Paul?

Colossians 1:24-29

I am glad when I suffer for you in my body, for I am participating in the sufferings of Christ that continue for his body, the church. (1:24)

He was a cosmopolitan guy, our Paul: Israelite by ancestry, Roman by citizenship, Jew by religion, and Greek by the culture of the times. He was highly educated and most probably fluent in at least three languages: Hebrew, Greek and Aramaic. His extensive writings reflect a classic Greek education as well as rabbinical training. He was someone who was so zealous in the pursuit of what he felt was right versus what he felt was wrong that he became the perfect agent to hunt down and eliminate the hated new religious sect that followed the crucified criminal known as Jesus of Nazareth. That is until Jesus Christ stopped him on the road to Damascus and literally turned his opinions around one hundred and eighty degrees.

Paul had quite a history. How much do you know about him?

1. What Israelite tribe was he descended from? (Romans 11:1) ______________________________
2. What was his profession by trade? (Acts 18:3) ______________________________
3. Whose murder did he witness? (Acts 7:54-60) ______________________________
4. What was Saul's initial goal regarding Jesus Christ's followers? (Acts 8:1-3) ______________________________
5. To get his attention, what handicap did God afflict Saul with for a brief period of time? (Acts 9) ______________________________
6. What was the name of the highly respected expert in religious law who taught Saul/Paul? (Acts 22:3) ______________________________

<u>Take the time to read Paul's Theology:</u>

"So now there is no condemnation for those who belong to Christ Jesus. [2] And because you belong to him, the power of the life-giving Spirit has freed you from the power of sin that leads to death. [3] The law of Moses was unable to save us because of the weakness of our sinful nature. So God did what the law could not do. He sent his own Son in a body like the bodies we sinners have. And in that body God declared an end to sin's control over us by giving his Son as a sacrifice for our sins. [4] He did this so that the just requirement of the law would be fully satisfied for us, who no longer follow our sinful nature but instead follow the Spirit." Romans 8:1-4

8. What distinguished religious group was Saul/Paul a part of? (Philippians 3:5)

   ____

9. By birth, Saul/Paul was a citizen of where? (Acts 22:27-28) ______________________________________

10. Write the number of times Paul endured each of the following (2 Corinthians 11:24-27):

    a. _____ received 39 lashes

    b. _____ beaten with rods

    c. _____ stoned

    d. _____ shipwrecked

    e. _____ adrift at sea for a day and night

WORD BANK: tent maker, Rome, Benjamin, blindness, Stephen, Gamaliel, Pharisee, destroy,

Paul claimed to be an apostle of Jesus Christ. Do you know that some people challenged him on that front? First, you have to know how an apostle is different from a disciple. An **apostle** was specifically "one of a group made up especially of the twelve disciples chosen by Jesus to preach the gospel" while a **disciple** is "one who embraces and assists in spreading the teachings of another." (Free Online Dictionary) In case you need further clarification, all apostles are disciples but all disciples are not apostles!

But, you might say, I don't think Paul ever physically met Jesus, did he?

Well, the answer to that question depends on how you look at things. While Jesus Christ walked in human form on earth Paul *did not* encounter him. But on the road to Damascus, he heard a voice from heaven that said, "I am Jesus the Nazarene, the one you are persecuting" (Acts 22:8) and from that conversation, Paul received his personal call to be an apostle from Jesus Christ. (I Corinthians 15:10)

What did Paul look like?

"...a man small in size, balk-headed, crooked thighs [note: bow-legged], well-built, with eyebrows meeting, rather long-nosed, full of grace. For sometimes he seemed like a man, and sometimes he had the countenance of an angel." (The Acts of Paul)

QUESTIONS:

What is Paul's responsibility? (1:25)

For whom was the secret revealed? (1:26b, 27a)

What was the secret? (1:27b)

What do believers have to assist them? (1:28a)

What is Paul's goal? (1:28b)

Where does our strength come from? (1:29)

Take the time to read:
*Paul's Conversion – Acts 22
*Paul's Prayer for Believers – Ephesians 3:14-21

Although Paul wrote the most books in the New Testament (13 – there is a question as to who actually wrote Hebrews so that's not in the count) Luke who wrote 'just' the books of Luke and Acts technically wrote more words than any other writer in the New Testament.

In art, Paul is often shown with a sword and a book which is believed to symbolize both the manner of his death (believed to be by beheading) and his writings which, by his own word, he described as the "sword of the spirit." (Ephesians 6:17)

PERSONAL THOUGHTS: Is my life a witness?

No one promised that our life as a believer would be easy. What hardships have you faced over the course of your life?

We are promised that even though we walk through the valley of the shadow of death God is with us. (Psalm 23) During your hardest times, can you pinpoint evidence of God's love and care for you?

When times are difficult, what avenues do you have in your life for spiritual, mental, and emotional support?

What are some things you can do <u>in preparation</u> for tough times?

Can you use the hardships in your life to further God's Kingdom on earth?

What are some of the images of Colossians 1?

"Christ as the Head ... the church as the body..."

Christ is also the head of the church, which is his body. (1:18a)

What is the mental image in Colossians 1? You should always take advantage of the visual images provided in the scripture that will help you understand and remember key points.

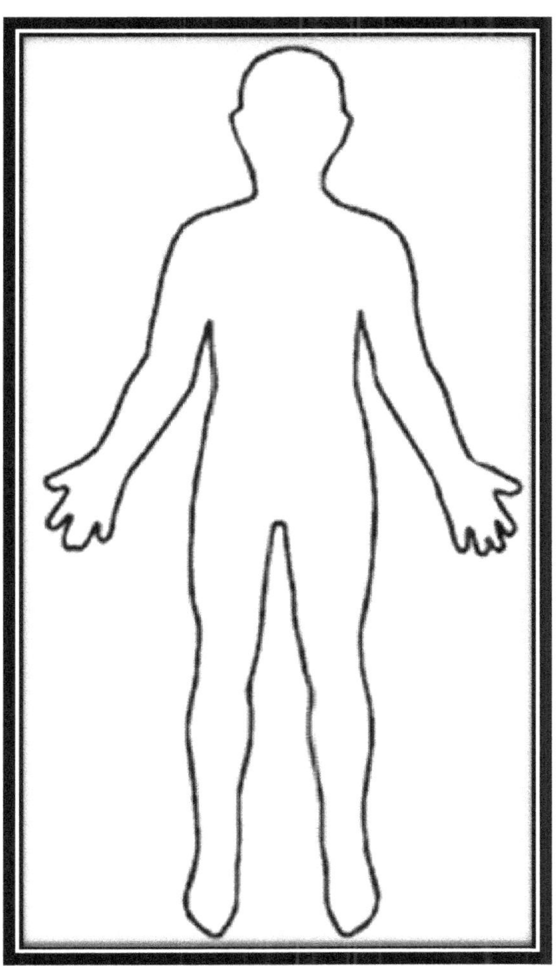

Think about this:

*What is the full implication of Colossians 1:18a?

*How does a head impact the body?

*Can the body ever 'overrule' the head?

*Can the body survive without the head?

*What happens to the body when the head becomes "divided"? (i.e. pulled in two or more directions)

*Can you explain how Jesus Christ is the head and the church is the body?

WALKING WITH JESUS: How does this apply to me and my church?

The Good News

For we have heard of your faith in Christ Jesus and your love for all of God's people, which come from your confident hope of what God has reserved for you in heaven. You have had this expectation ever since you first heard the truth of the Good News. (1:5)

1. How does your church articulate the Good News of Jesus Christ? (Does it have a Statement of Faith? Does it have a Mission Statement?)

2. How do you articulate the Good News of Jesus Christ? (Do you have a Statement of Faith?)

Sharing The News

This same Good News that came to you is going out all over the world. It is bearing fruit everywhere by changing lives, just as it changed your lives from the day you first heard and understood the truth about God's wonderful grace. (1:6)

3. List the key things that your church does to spread the Good News to the world.

4. What role do you play in spreading the Good News to the world?

Prayer

We also pray that you will be strengthened with all his glorious power so you will have all the endurance and patience you need. (1:11)

5. What are specific things that need to be prayed about regarding your church's ministry?

6. What are specific things that need to be prayed about regarding you and your witness to the world?

A Life In Jesus Christ

Christ lives in you. (1:27b)

7. What evidence is there that your church is filled with the Holy Spirit and successfully working toward spreading the Gospel?

8. What evidence is there that Christ lives in you and that He is the primary focus in your life?

9. How do you explain to others what Jesus Christ means to you?

The Head and Body

...for I am participating in the sufferings of Christ that continue for his body, the church. (1:24)

10. What part of the body are you?

11. How do you stay connected to the Head?

12. How do you stay attuned to the other parts of the body that may need you?

PERSONAL THOUGHTS: What is your church's mission?

What is your church's mission statement?

How do you fit in to your church's mission statement?

Chapter 2: WALKING IN COMPLETENESS

Therefore he is able, once and forever, to save those who come to God through him. He lives forever to intercede with God on their behalf. Hebrews 7:25

Questions worth considering as you read and study Colossians 2:

1. What are the keys to success for believers?
2. What must I do to be complete?
3. What were some of the beliefs of the time?
4. What are some mental images of Colossians 2?
5. How does this apply to me and my church?

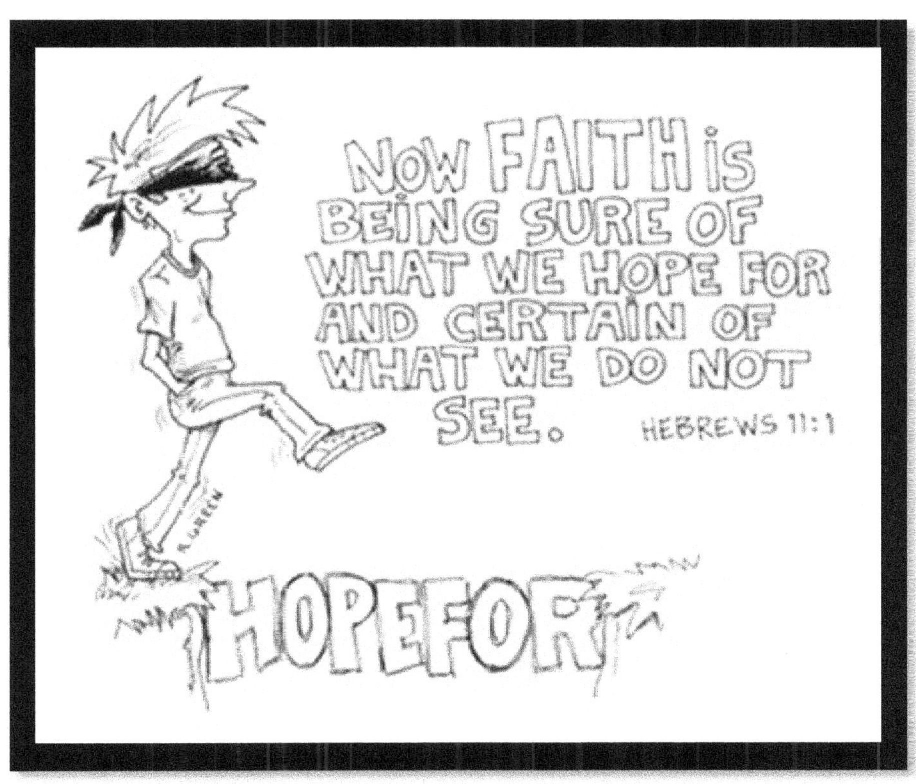

What are the keys to success for believers?

Colossians 2:1-7

And I rejoice that you are living as you should and that your faith in Christ is strong. (2:5b)

Paul begins chapter two of Colossians with words of encouragement for success. What is your recipe for success in life? Personally? Professionally? Spiritually? In their May 15, 2014, issue *Time* magazine writer Jeffrey Pfeffer identified six traits that were keys to success in high achievers:

1. Energy and Physical Stamina
2. Focus
3. Sensitivity to Others
4. Flexibility
5. Ability to Tolerate Conflict
6. Submerging One's Ego and Getting Along

Of course Paul and Pfeffer had different opinions about what constituted success! While all the above traits would certainly be acceptable considerations, Paul urged a different set of traits for a believer's success. Believers should:

1. Be encouraged and knit together with strong ties of ______________________________ (2:2a)
2. Have complete ______________________________ that they understand God's mysterious plan. (2:2b)
3. Making use of all the treasures of wisdom and knowledge which is found only in ______________________________ (2:3)
4. Have accepted Christ Jesus as Lord, and must continue to ______________________________ (2:6)
5. Let their faith grow strong in the ______________________________ (2:7)
6. Overflow with ______________________________ (2:7 b)

"We cannot be built up in Christ, or grow in Him, unless we are first rooted in Him, or founded upon Him." (Henry, 1435)

A grounding, growing, grateful believer will not be led astray. (Wiersbe, 75)

"Knowledge and faith make a rich soul." (Henry, 1435)

"Everything, then, must be in Christ if all the fullness of the Godhead dwells in him!...In Christ we enter into the fullness and completeness of life both materially and spiritually." (Spurgeon, Loc 139)

WORD BANK: truth, love, thankfulness, follow, confidence, Christ

QUESTION: Of Paul's six keys for success for believers, in which areas are you the strongest? The weakest?

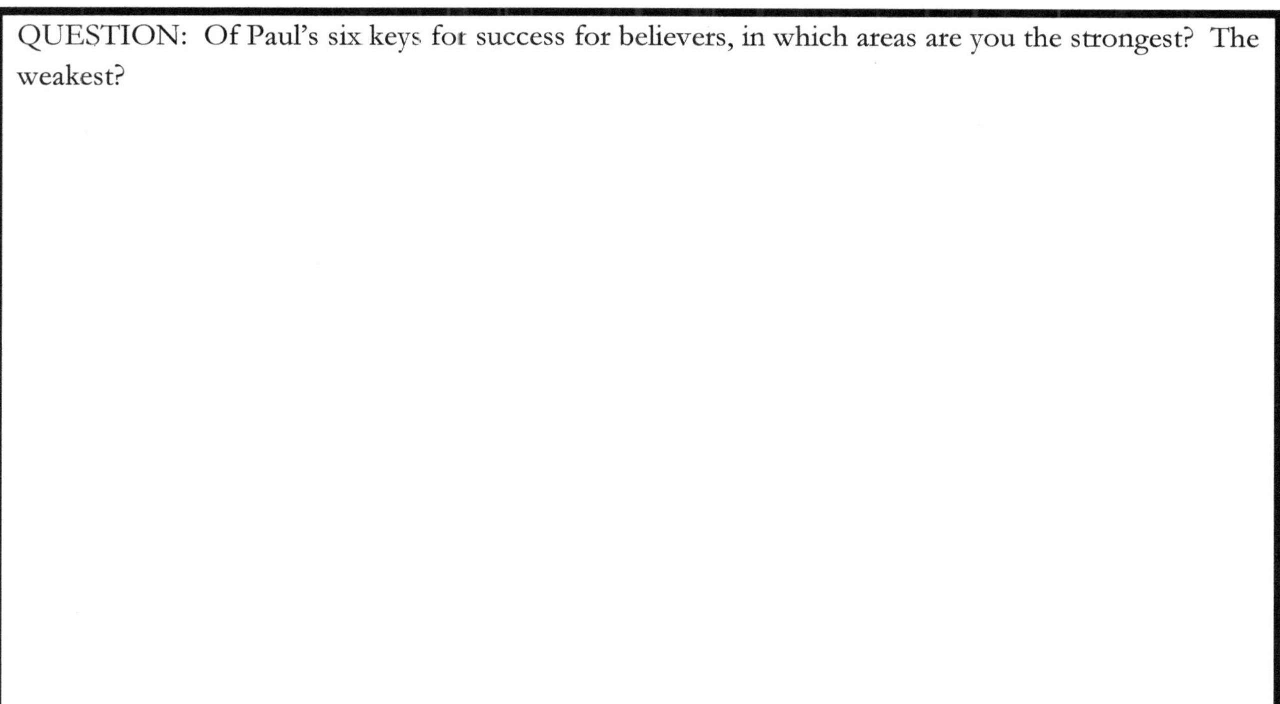

PERSONAL THOUGHTS: My Success Plan

What is your personal plan for spiritual success?

What must I do to be complete?

Colossians 2:8-17

For in Christ lives all the fullness of Good in a human body. So you are complete through your union with Christ, who is the head over every ruler and authority. (2:9-10)

Sin separates us from God. What must we do to bridge the divide? How can we repair what has been broken and make us complete in God's eyes once again?

The first attempt to do this was offered to the Jews by God through Moses. The entire life of a Jewish person was controlled by this Mosaic Law. Summarized in the Ten Commandments (Exodus 20), the Jewish leaders added even more rules in an earnest attempt to achieve perfection (holiness) in God's eyes. Take a moment to look at the table below.

Earthly Inheritance Through the Mosaic Law	Spiritual Inheritance Through Christ
Was External behaviors	Is Internal belief
Involved circumcision – a physical procedure	Involved a spiritual circumcision – the cutting away of our sinful nature. (2:11)
Buried in death.	Buried with Christ through baptism and raised in new life. (2:12)
Death inevitable because of our sinful nature	Eternal Life promised because of Christ's forgiveness of sins. (2:13-14)
Trapped by sin. Our sin cannot be eradicated.	Freed through belief in Christ.
Restricted through the rules of eating, drinking, holy days.	Free through Christ's sacrifice. (2:16-17)
Rules are the reality.	Christ is the reality.

The Mosaic Law, AKA:
*The Law
*The Old Covenant
*The Law of Moses
*The Torah
*The Pentateuch

"You have everything in Christ that you ought to need. You are fully furnished, completely supplied, and equipped for all future service." (Spurgeon Loc 144)

"To be complete is to be furnished with all things necessary for salvation. (Henry, 1436)

"By this one word complete, is shown that we have in Christ whatever is required." (Henry, 1436)

"Jesus not only took our sins to the cross (I Peter 2:24), but He also too the Law to the cross and nailed it there forever out of the way." (Wiersbe, 82)

Christ said at the Last Supper, "This cup is the new covenant between God and his people—an agreement confirmed with my blood, which is poured out as a sacrifice for you." (Luke 22:20) His death on the cross moved us from The Mosaic Law Covenant to the new covenant which was sealed with his blood. No longer were just the Jews privileged to know the One True God; the new covenant that Jesus Christ instituted opened the door for <u>anyone</u> who believed.

QUESTION: What problems can you foresee between faithful Jews who became followers of Jesus Christ and Gentiles who also began to follow Jesus Christ?

The freedom that Jesus Christ offered to all believers – Jews and Gentiles alike – was something never heard of before. Just believe and you were *in?* Just request forgiveness and you were *forgiven?* Some of those faithful Jews who found joy in recognizing Jesus Christ as their promised Messiah had … problems with this freedom. What about the Holy Days? What about the eating restrictions? What about blood sacrifices? What about the Sabbath? What about circumcision? *What about The Mosaic Law??* Many Jews just could not shed a lifetime of practices any more than they could they allow the Gentiles to stand side by side with them and be seen as equal in God's eyes. False teachers began to insist that unless you followed The Mosaic Law you could not be a true believer in Jesus Christ.

Paul, expertly educated and intimately familiar with all the strictures of The Law, was the perfect person to deal with this difficult topic. Over and over again in his letters (to not only the Colossians but the Romans and the Corinthians) he argued the

<u>Gentiles</u> – anyone who was not a Jew. The word carried with us a connotation of someone who was barbaric and uncivilized.

"Let no man beguile you of your reward." (1:18)

"Why are you subject to such ordinances of men when Christ has set you free from them all?" (Spurgeon, Loc 189)

"Do not make yourself subject to the judgment of other men." (Spurgeon, Loc 164)

See more comments by Paul on this subject: Romans 10, Romans 14:5, I Corinthians 8, Galatians 3:22-25, Ephesians 2:15

truth of Jesus Christ: that in Him was all the fullness of God in a human body (2:9) and through our belief in Christ, believers too were now complete (2:10) A follower of Jesus Christ need do nothing else to achieve salvation but believe these things.

PERSONAL THOUGHTS: On Being Complete

What aspects of your faith are essential for you to feel complete? Holy? Spiritual? Connected to God?

Are you open or closed to new ideas within your church? What is your baseline for deciding?

How do you gauge if something is "right" or "wrong"?

Within your realm of friends and acquaintances, who do you trust when it comes to advice? What were the criteria you used to come to this decision?

What were some of the beliefs of the time?

Colossians 2:16-23

Just like we cope with different beliefs today, there were many religions bombarding the Colossae Christians. Mysticism, the occult, philosophy, and the worship of angels were common and while all were concerns, based on Paul's letter it would seem that the primary points of trouble were Jewish Legalism and Gnosticism. Let's talk about these two.

Jewish Legalism

Jewish Legalism emphasized the letter of the law at the expense of the spirit. It emphasized discipline of conduct and legal ideas and did not take into account God's mercy and grace. There were some Jewish followers of Christ who simply could not set aside the ancient customs and practices of their Jewish heritage and *insisted* that without the continued observance of these rules believers in Christ could not be saved. They maintained that the Law of Moses could not be replaced by belief in Jesus Christ but taught that *both* needed to be observed.

The Las of Moses:

- Given only to the Jews.
- Was given as a mark of God's favor, but was also a yoke to the Jews.
- Was a way to ratify their covenant with God while at the same time established a wall which excluded the Gentiles.
- Condemned all to death because of sin. (Cursed is anyone who does not affirm and obey the terms of these instructions. Deuteronomy 27:26)

Philosophia – Greek word which refers to everything from the metaphysics of Plato to the religious teaching of cults. (Strongs, #5385) (It should be noted that Paul's issue with philosophy was rooted in those philosophical speculations that stood opposed to the Good News, not philosophy in general.)

Mysticism – otherworldly practices involving mysteries known only to those who are initiated. These mysteries transcend ordinary human knowledge and seek direct communication with the divine or otherworldly beings.

Occult – supernatural, mystical, or magical beliefs, practices, or phenomena.

- Was originally written by Moses (summarized with the 10 Commandments **The Law** is detailed in the first five books of the Bible – aka **The Torah** or the **Pentateuch**). Over the centuries, Jewish rabbis had added many additional laws in an attempt to keep themselves from breaking the Law. Many of these 'added' laws often actually caused obstacles to obeying God's rules. (See Mark 7:1-15)
- Was incorrectly believed to automatically please God when Jews attempted to abide by it. Observance of the Sabbath and holy days was absolutely essential. (2:16) Circumcision was thought to help with spiritual development. (2:11) Dietary laws were useful in attaining spiritual perfection. (2:14-17) Rules regarding what was evil and what was good were essential. (2:21) Rigid discipline was required to be spiritual right. (2:23)

Jesus Christ:

- Was the 'New Covenant' first referred to in Jeremiah 31:31-34 and verified by Christ in Luke 22:20.
- Was the final, perfect sacrifice. (Romans 6:3-7)
- Changed the Sabbath to now being a remembrance of His resurrection. (2:16-17)
- Cancelled the requirements of the Law through his death, burial, and resurrection by fulfilling it. Salvation is now a free gift. (Ephesians 2:8-9) (2:20) (Matthew 5:17-18, Romans 10:4, Hebrews 9:12)
- Delivered all believers from the sentence of death of the Law. (2:20-21)

"All the Mosaic ceremonies from which you were shut out as Gentiles are abolished!" (Spurgeon, Loc 154)

The word "**Talmud**" is a Hebrew word meaning "learning, instruction." The Talmud is a central text of mainstream Judaism and consists primarily of discussions and commentary on Jewish history, law (especially its practical application to life), customs and culture. The Talmud consists of what are known as the Gemara and the Mishnah. The Talmud is also known as "The Oral Torah."

The New Covenant through Jesus Christ:
*Free for anyone who believes
*Frees all from the penalty of The Law
*Gifts all who believe with the Holy Spirit who dwells within us
*Provides a direct, permanent, unbreakable relationship with God.

- Was now the only essential reality all believers needed to follow. (2:17) (Mark 7:18-19)
- Was the center of **true piety** - religious, reverent behavior. (2:16)
- Cancelled the need of the priesthood being intermediaries between God and man and now offers believers a permanent, unbroken relationship with God through the Holy Spirit who lives in all believers. (Romans 8:9-10, Hebrews 9:15) (2:19) (John 4:21-23, Matthew 18:20)
- Freed us from all spiritual powers of this world. (2:20)
- Freed us from all human rules and teachings. (2:20-22)

Gnosticism

The word **Gnostic** is from the Greek word **gnosis** which means "to know". A gnostic is a person "in the know" when it came to deep things of God. A gnostic is a 'spiritual aristocrat' in the church who works toward spiritual perfection and depth and is only achieved by a select few. (Strongs, #1108)

Gnostics Believe:

- Matter is inherently evil and that spirit is good. As a result of this belief, Gnostics believe that anything done in the body, even the grossest sin, has no meaning because real life exists in the spirit realm only. This causes them to approach life in one of two ways. Either they practices **asceticism** which is an extreme form of self-denial and austerity *or* **licentiousness** which is a complete lack of moral restraint especially regarding sexual conduct. (Think wantonness, looseness, self-indulgence…) Sin isn't the problem, ignorance is. (Romans 3:23)

What are the "rules" of the New Covenant? (See Acts 16:31 if you don't know the answer!)

"For the law was given through Moses, but God's unfailing love and faithfulness came through Jesus Christ." John 1:17

Gnostics of today may be part of a cult group known as the "Theosophical Society" which focuses on ancient Gnosticism as well as Hinduism and Christianity. This title is based in the Greek word **theosophia** which means literally "divine wisdom." (Martin, 281) The motto of the society is "There is no religion higher than truth."

Famous "Modern Day" Gnostics:
*Tori Amos – musician
*Carl Jung – psychologist
*William Butler Yeats – poet
*Leo Tolstoy - author

- Salvation is gained through the acquisition of divine knowledge which frees one from the illusions of darkness. It is not available to everyone but rather just a select group who received a special revelation. Man's spirit which is suffering imprisonment in the material body will be freed upon death. This is a direct contradiction of Jesus' teachings which stated, "God saved you by his grace when you believed. And you can't take credit for this; it is a gift from God. Salvation is not a reward for the good things we have done, so none of us can boast about it." (Ephesians 2:8-9, John 11:25, John 3:18, John 6:40)
- In a variety of early heretical writings known as the Gnostic gospels which are regularly claimed to be "lost books of the Bible." These documents give false doctrines about Jesus Christ, salvation, God, and every other crucial Christian truth. (John 14:6)
- That Jesus' physical body was not real, but only "seemed" to be physical. His spirit descended upon Him at His baptism, but left Him just before His crucifixion. The biblical view of Jesus is that He was completely human as well as fully God. (John 1:18, Galatians 4:4, Matthew 16:15-16, Philippians 2:10-11)
- Is into the mystical, intuitive, subjective, inward, emotional approach to truth. God's Word is false and is the product of man, not God. (John 14:6, Proverbs 3:5-7, I Peter 3:13-15)
- In reincarnation. There will be no physical resurrection of the body. (John 11:25-26)
- Various manifestations of "God." Some even allow for a father god and a mother goddess. (Genesis 17:1, Isaiah 55:8-9)
- That they are seekers more than believers and that questioning one's faith is always important for it to change and grow. They shun the material world and embrace the spiritual world.

(SEE THE APPENDIX at the back of this book which has detailed information on a variety of current religions of today: Judaism, Scientology, Jehovah's Witness, Mormon, Hindu, Christian Science, Islam, and The Occult.)

Reincarnation – the theological belief that on the death of the body the soul transmigrates to or is born again in another body.

QUESTION: What specific behaviors were the Colossae believers being condemned for? (2:16-23)

QUESTION: What other faiths do you contend with on a daily basis with friends, colleagues, and strangers?

How can you share your faith with others without offending or insulting them? Do you even try?

"Jesus won complete victory over all satanic powers. Circumnavigating Jesus Christ substitutes superstition for revelation and denies the Person and work of Jesus Christ."
(Wiersbe, 12-13)

"When we make Jesus Christ and the Christian revelation only <u>part</u> of a total religious system or philosophy, we cease to give Him the preeminence."
(Wiersbe, 13)

<u>The wrong way to think:</u>

"God is far away, matter is evil, and demonic forces are constantly threatening us."

<u>The right way to think:</u>

"God is near us, God made all things good (although they can be used for evil) and Christ has delivered us from the powers of darkness."
(Wiersbe, 14)

PERSONAL THOUGHTS: You & The World

What are some responses you could use regarding people who:

Don't recognize The Bible as God's inspired word?

Don't feel the need to attend church worship on a regular basis?

Don't believe that prayer works?

Don't believe in God and/or Jesus Christ?

Personal stories are the most powerful weapon against those who doubt Jesus Christ. What aspects of your life are you willing to share that illustrate God's love and care for you?

What are some of the images of Colossians 2?

A solidly rooted tree

Let your roots grow down into him, and let your lives be built on him. (2:7)

Think about this:

*What connotations are implied by being compared to a 'well rooted tree'?

*What other objects in nature would be an equivalent comparison?

*What are we to be 'rooted in'?

*Read some other references to "roots": Ephesians 3:17, Colossians 2:7, Jeremiah 17:7-8, Psalm 1:3, Psalm 92:12-14 Is the imagery consistent?

Dead, buried, and resurrected

You were dead because of your sins… Then God made you alive with Christ… (2:13-14)

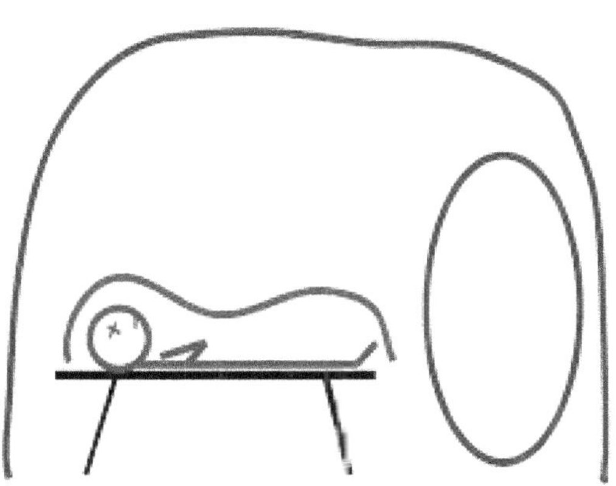

Think about this:

*Read Leviticus 17:11, I John 1:7, Hebrews 9:12-14. Do these passages help you further understand the magnitude of Christ's sacrifice on the cross?

*Can you understand the future imagery of the Old Testament sacrifices for sins? (Leviticus 1::-7:38)

*What is the implication of us being dead, buried and resurrected with Christ?

WALKING IN COMPLETENESS: How does this apply to me and my church?

On Being Complete

And now, just as you accepted Christ Jesus as your Lord, you must continue to follow him. (2:6)

1. What opportunities does your church offer in order to grow in your new life in Jesus Christ?

2. What causes you your greatest spiritual growth?

3. What aspects of your life cause you the greatest spiritual fulfillment in your new life?

4. What areas of your life cause the greatest struggle between your new life and your old life?

Chapter 3: WALKING IN NEW LIFE

Throw off your old sinful nature and your former way of life, which is corrupted by lust and deception. Instead, let the Spirit renew your thoughts and attitudes. Put on your new nature, created to be like God—truly righteous and holy.
Ephesians 4:22-24

Questions to consider as you read Colossians 3:

1. What does a new life in Christ mean?
2. What is Paul's Household Code?
3. What are the mental images of Colossians 3?
4. How does this apply to me and my church?

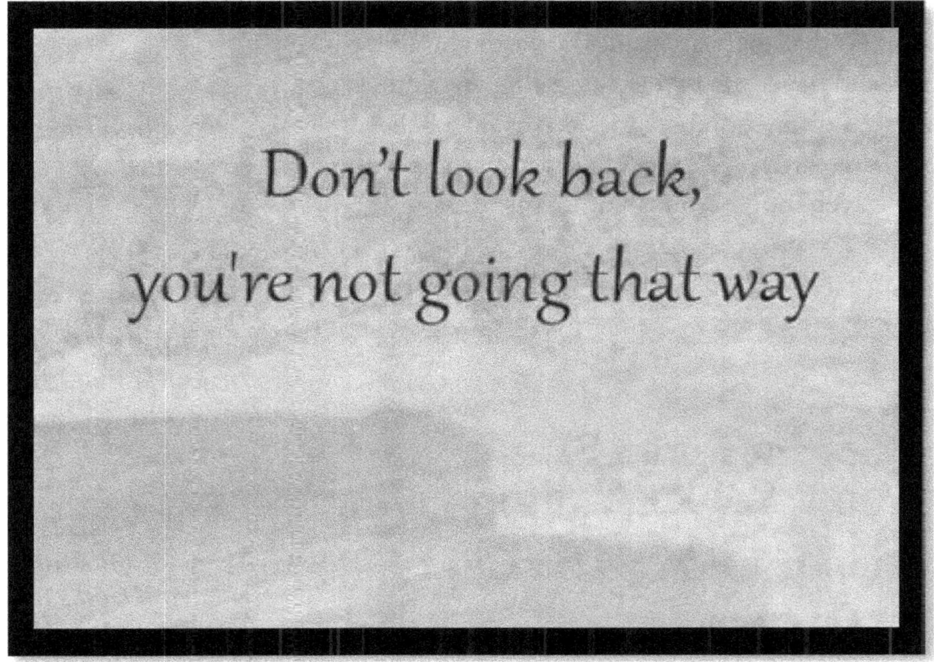

What does a new life in Christ mean?

Colossians 3:1-11

Think about the things of heaven, not the things of earth. 3:2

C.S. Lewis calls it spiritual evolution: that point in a person's life where he or she goes from being an unbeliever to a believer. Lewis actually claims that it is only through this evolution that we become a *real human being*, i.e. the type of creation that God always intended us to be. That change causes us to become entirely new creatures! Paul said it perfectly in 2 Corinthians 5:17, "This means that anyone who belongs to Christ has become a new person. The old life is gone; a new life has begun!"

The reality is that there are things of earth and there are things of heaven and never the two shall meet. A new life found in Christ means that distinction becomes central in a believer's life and the things of earth fade away. Paul says we are to think about things of heaven, not the things of earth. (3:2)

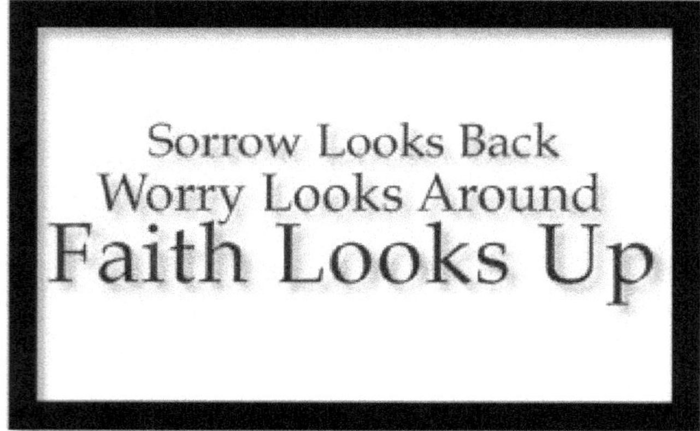

The following two illustrations attempt to show the "spiritual evolution" that C.S. Lewis spoke of.

"Heaven and earth are contrary to one another." (Henry, 1437)

<u>Glorified</u> - To give glory, honor, or high praise to; exalt.

"Live above." (Spurgeon, Loc 207)

"Very often we are seeking the things below as if we have not yet attained new life..." (Spurgeon Loc 203)

<u>Idolater</u> – someone who worships things of the world.

"We are <u>formed</u> in God's image and <u>deformed</u> from God's image by sin. But through Jesus Christ we can be <u>transformed</u> into God's image." (Wiersbe, 108)

"There is now no difference from country, or conditions, and circumstances of life." (Henry, 1438)

C.S. Lewis says that the ordinary way that life progresses is derived from others (our ancestors) regarding the very odd, very confusing process known as sex. Our new life with Christ involves belief, baptism, and the Holy Spirit. We cannot see how these three things spread the Christ life in us but they are as "odd" or as unexplainable as how sex works!

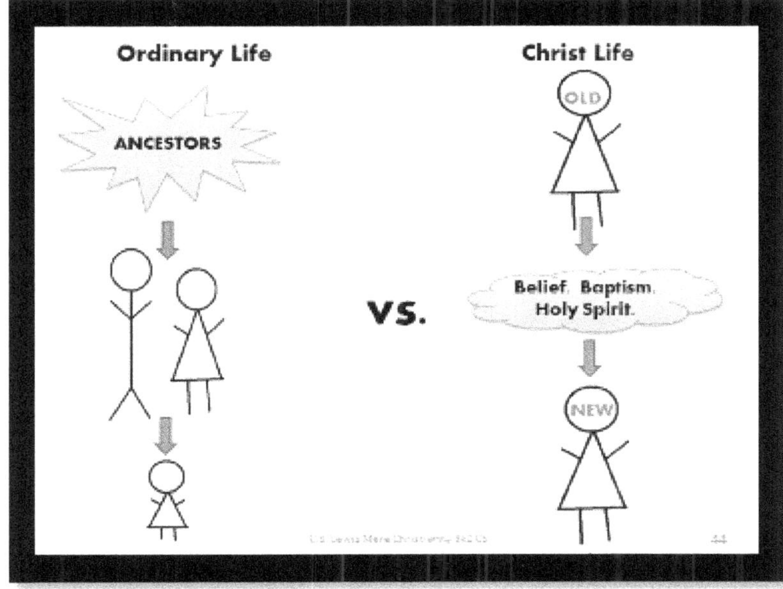

Again, C.S. Lewis says that with (The Trinity) Christ beside us helping us, with the Holy Spirit within us helping us, and with the Father above us helping us we can begin to change from a "stick figure" (something that is just a vague imitation of what God intended us to be) into a Real Human.

"Jesus Christ was The Perfect Human Being... He was one human that was really what all humans were intended to be." (Lewis)

"With Christ beside us helping us, with the Holy Spirit within us helping us, with the Father above us helping us, we can begin to change from a ... stick figure becoming a ... Real Human. (Lewis)

Our New Life: What We Now Are

Paul tried to explain this to the Colossians, too. According to Paul, the new life in Christ means that:

1. We are ______________________________ with Christ. (3:1a)
2. We are ______________________________ on the realities of heaven. (3:1b)
3. We are ______________________________ about the things of heaven. (3:2)
4. We ______________________________ with Christ. (3:3a)
5. We are ______________________________ in Christ. (3:3b)
6. We ______________________________ in Christ. (3:4a)
7. We are ______________________________ in Christ. (3:4b)
8. We are ______________________________ as we learn about Christ. (3:10)
9. We are culturally ______________________ in Christ. (3:11)
10. We are ______________________________ Jesus Christ because he lives in all of us. (3:10)

Word Bank: died, renewed, raised, live, hidden, thinking, glorified, focused, indistinguishable, like

"We must not only do no hurt to any, but do what good we can to all." (Henry, 1438)

Our New Life: What We Aren't Anymore

The struggle for every believer is separating themselves from the evils found within the earthly life. Just in case you aren't sure what those evils are, Paul takes the time to make a list.

List all the sinful, earthly behaviors that we are to put to death as a result of our new life in Christ. (3:5-11)

Our New Life: What We Need To Be For Others

Paul said it over and over again: as Believers we are called to tell others about the Good News of Jesus Christ. "Let the message about Christ, in all its richness, fill your lives." (3:16) This message of The Truth that we carry isn't necessarily just words; it's actions, too.

What behaviors will you exhibit when Christ fills your life? (3:12-17)

PERSONAL THOUGHTS: The Old & The New

Sometimes one of the hardest things is actually believing that the "old" is gone and forgotten and that we are new, transformed creatures.

How does your old life compare with your new?

What areas shine?

What areas still need work?

What is Paul's Household Code?

Colossians 3:18-25, 4:1

For God has no favorites. (3:25b)

"Wives, submit to your husbands…" That line has been one of the single most controversial Bible verses in the Bible and has caused people inaccurately to claim that the apostle Paul seems to hate women.

Women had a large place in Jesus' ministry and Paul supported that. The truth was "the most striking thing about the role of women in the life and teaching of Jesus is the simple fact that they were there. Although the gospel texts contain no special sayings repudiating the view of the day about women, their uniform testimony to the presence of women among the followers of Jesus and to his serious teaching of them constitutes a break with tradition which has been described as being 'without precedent in [then] contemporary Judaism." (Hurley, 82, 83)

Christ's ministry radically changed the world of women in his day. At a time when only boys were educated, at a time when women were excluded from all but the necessary parts of their faith required to keep a kosher home, at a time when women were valued only for their ability to produce male children, Jesus's ministry began.

Paul's household code attempted to give solid advice as to how to run a home. He spoke of it in Colossians and in Ephesians 5 and Peter spoke of it in I Peter 3.

1. Wives are to ______________________________ to their husbands as it is fitting for those who belong to the Lord. (3:18)
2. Husbands are to ______________________________ and never treat their wives ______________________________. (3:19)
3. Children are to ______________________________ their parents. (3:20)
4. Fathers are not to ______________________________ their children. (3:21)

Submit – to recognize one's place under someone else in a social order. Such submission always implies that God is at the top and that His Will is paramount. (NLT, 3:18 notes)

Submission – not slavery or subjugation; more like military rank. (Wiersbe, 124)

Love – **agape** – the sacrificing serving love that Jesus Christ shares with His church. (Strong's, #26)

Obey – to carry out or fulfill a command, order, or instruction.

Paul also addressed this topic in I Peter 2:18-3:7 and Ephesians 5:22-6:9

Submit to one another out of reverence for Christ. Ephesians 5:21

"Let us deal with servants as we expect God to deal with us."

5. Slaves are to ______________________________ their masters. (3:22)
6. Masters must be ___________________________ and ______________________________. To their slaves. (4:1)
7. Masters are to remember that they have a ______________________________ in heaven. (4:1)

WORD BANK: obey, Master, love, fair, aggravate, just, submit, harshly,

Look at this fascinating list of events regarding Jesus and Women! (Please take the time to notice how many of these events are "firsts"!)

- Jesus welcomed women followers (Luke 8:1-3)
- Jesus taught women (Luke 10:39, John 4)
- Jesus allowed women to be disciples (Matthew 12:46-50)
- Jesus had women who financially support Him during His ministry: Joanna, the wife of Chuza, Susanna, "and many others" (Luke 8:3)
- Jesus regularly used women in his parables and illustrations (Luke 8:1-8, Luke 21:1-4, Luke 15:8-10),
- Jesus defended women (Matthew 5:27-32)
- Jesus pronounced forgiveness to prostitutes (Luke 7:36-50)
- First Person To Know That He Was Coming: Mary (Luke 1:30-32)
- First Person To Profess Faith In Him: Elizabeth (Luke 1:42-43)
- First Person To Proclaim Him to the World: Anna (Luke 2:36-38)
- Longest Recorded Conversation Between Jesus and a Person: The Woman of Samaria (John 4:1-42)

<u>Question</u>: If Jesus obviously had a progressive attitude towards women and their role in the church, why didn't the early church take a harder line to promote this?

<u>Answer</u>: The purpose of the early church was to spread the Gospel and not to get involved with social action. See I Corinthians 7:21

- First Person That Jesus Reveals His True Identity As The Messiah To: The Woman of Samaria (John 4:1-42)
- First Person To Anoint Christ: The Sinful Woman (Luke 7:36-50)
- First Person To Be Healed Through Touching Christ: The Woman With The Issue of Blood (Matt 9:20-22, Mark 5:25-34, Luke 8:43-48)
- Earthly Home/Place of Rest for Jesus: Martha of Bethany's home (Luke 10:38-42)
- First Person to Express Knowledge/Sorrow of Jesus' Impending Death: Mary of Bethany (Mark 14:7-8)
- Only Person Christ Pronounced Immortal Fame Over Because Of A Specific Deed: Mary of Bethany and her anointing of Christ (Mark 14:3-9)
- Witnesses of Christ's Death/Present at The Crucifixion: Mary (Mother of Jesus), Mary Magdalene, Salome (Zebedee's wife and the mother of James and John), Mary (The wife of Clopas and mother of James the younger and Joseph), John the disciple (John 19:25)
- Only Person At Every Scene Related To Jesus' Crucifixion and Resurrection: Mary Magdalene
- First Person The Risen Jesus Christ Appeared To and Spoke To: Mary Magdalene (Mark 16:9, John 20:11-18))
- First People To Know Of The Resurrection: Mary Magdalene, Joanna, and Mary the mother of James (Luke 24:1-10)
- First Human Heralds of the Resurrection: Mary Magdalene, Joanna, and Mary the mother of James (Luke 24:1-10)
- First Person To Be Told By Christ To Herald the Resurrection: Mary Magdalene (John 20:17)

Jesus may not have spoken openly about his intention to change the status of women in society, but his actions certainly did.

Paul's mission was to further the ministry of Jesus Christ, not change it. In reality, when Paul admonished women to "submit to their husbands," he wasn't trying to *undo* what Jesus had started but was trying to further it. Paul's letters almost always addressed issues and concerns within specific churches and obviously the churches of Ephesus and Colossae had some issues regarding women and their place within worship. Yes, Paul told *some* women to ask their husbands if they had questions, to be silent in the church, to not teach men yet Paul *never* forbade women from learning, worshipping, serving, or teaching. he merely tries to structure where it happens.

- Paul encouraged women to ask their husbands and instructed husbands to teach their wives. (I Corinthians 14:35) It is important to remember that at this time period it was only the men who had been formally educated, why not take advantage of that? Were women asking too many disruptive questions in public? Were they upsetting the worship service with their curiosity? This needed to stop but the learning *did not.*

- Paul's First Convert in Europe and First Member of the Church of Philippi was Lydia. (Acts 16:6-40) He also greets Nympha (4:15) who has a church that meets in her house. If he was not in favor of women in authority positions, would he have encouraged either of these women?
- Paul worked with Priscilla and her husband Aquila tent making referring to them as "my fellow workers in Christ Jesus" (Romans 16:3). It is interesting to note that Priscilla is always listed first in his references to them.
- Paul's admonition on women to be silent in church (I Corinthians 14:34, I Timothy 2:12) apparently is temporary as he gives instructions on a woman's appearance when she prays and prophesies (I Corinthians 11:5). Why would he give instructions if he felt all women should be silent in church?
- Paul's stand on women not teaching men also seems to be temporary as his friend and colleague Priscilla and her husband Aquila jointly educated Apollos when he did not know the full extent of Jesus Christ's ministry. (Acts 18:24-26)

"The Gospel radically changed the position of women in the Roman world. It gave them a new freedom and stature that some of them were unable to handle and for this reason Paul admonished them." (Wiersbe, 124) Paul, in establishing the hierarchy that he did (God-husbands-wives-children-servants) greatly improved the conditions of women!

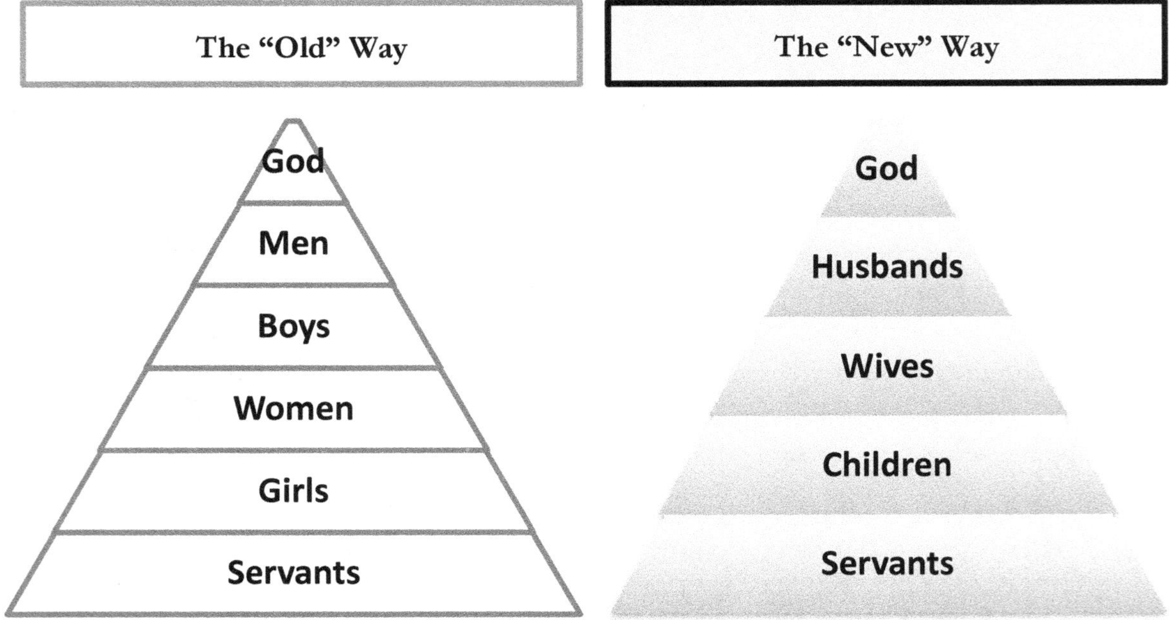

PERSONAL THOUGHT: Where Do You Stand?

What is your opinion regarding the role of wives submitting to their husbands? How do you support your stand?

What is your opinion regarding women and their roles in the church? How do you support your stand?

If you have children, what are the strongest examples you are showing them?

What are some of the images of Colossians 3?

A New Set of Clothes

"Stripped of your old…" (3:9)

"Put on your new…" (3:10)

"You must clothe yourselves…" (3:12)

"Above all, clothe yourselves with love…" (3:14)

Think about this:

*What do clothes say about a person?

*What opinions are drawn by a person's appearance?

*What image is created by the phrase, "Strip off your old…"?

*What illusion is created with the image of putting on "new clothes."

*What are the 'new' clothes that we are urged to 'put on'?

WALKING IN NEW LIFE: How does this apply to me and my church?

Heaven

…set your sights on the realities of heaven… (3:1)

1. What does your church do to encourage you to keep your sights on heaven?

2. What are some activities you participate on to keep your sights on heaven?

3. What are your realities of heaven?

Earth

So put to death the sinful, earthly things (3:5)

4. What earthly things interfere with church activities?

5. What earthly things interfere with your new life?

6. How do you work to put God first in your life?

Relationships

God chose you to be the holy people he loves… (3:12)

7. How does your new life effect your relationships:
   a. At work?

   b. With friends?

   c. With your spouse?

   d. With your children?

   e. With your extended family?

8. What new relationships does church offer you?

9. What opportunities does your church offer for fellowship?

9. What activities at church do you most enjoy?

10. What activities do you wish your church offered?

11. What activities outside of church do you enjoy? How has your new life influenced that area of your life?

12. Does your church empower you? Recognize you spiritual gifts? How? If not, why not?

Chapter 4: WALKING IN PRAYER

Pray without ceasing, I Thessalonians 5:17

Questions to consider as your read Colossians 4:

1. What are the essentials qualities of a New Life in Christ?
2. What happened to the Apostle Paul?
3. What are some mental images of Colossians 4?
4. How does this apply to me and my church?

Why do I pray?

Prayer does not fit us for the greater work; prayer is the greater work.

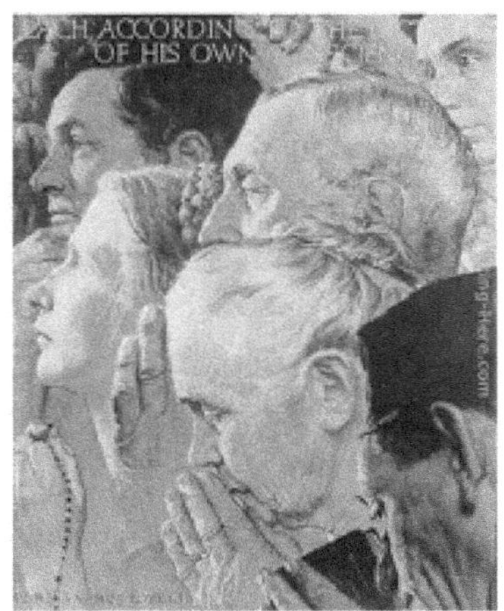

What are the essentials qualities of a New Life in Christ?

Colossians 4:2-6

Devote yourselves to prayer … (4:2)

1. When we pray we should have what two things? (4:2)

2. What two things should we ask for when we pray? (4:3, 4)

3. What two things should we do as we live with unbelievers? (4:5)

4. What two things should be reflected in our conversation? (4:6)

WORD BANK: graciousness, proclaim the message clearly, live wisely, alert mind, thankful heart, opportunities to speak, make the most of every opportunity, attractiveness,

"No duties can be done aright, unless we persevere in fervent prayers, and watch therein with thanksgiving." (Henry, 1439)

"A prayerless soul is a Christless soul. Prayer is the lisping of the believing infant, the shout of the fighting believer, the requiem of the dying saint falling asleep in Jesus." (Spurgeon Loc 266)

"Prayer and worship are perhaps the highest uses of the gift of speech." (Wiersbe, 136)

"Right conduct towards unbelievers. Recommend religion by all fit means. Carelessness may cause a lasting prejudice against the truth." (Henry, 1439)

Prayer: constantly, fervently, personally, definitely, sacrificially. (Wiersbe, 152-154)

What happened to the Apostle Paul?

Colossians 4:7-18

Remember my chains. (4:18)

Most of Paul's letters end with a series of greetings and references to co-workers, but here in the book of Colossians he spends a longer than usual time acknowledging those who have helped and supported him. Trapped in prison, he probably has great concern (and great frustration) over his inability to travel and communicate directly with those he cared about. Try to imagine your life, suddenly confined in your home without the convenience of telephone, Internet, or television. Who would you miss? Who would you worry about? How would you cope with the isolation? Who would become essential to your peace of mind and sanity? That is the situation that Paul was in.

Paul was permitted to be housed in his own rented place, although he was bound with a chain, and in the company of a guard. (Acts 28:16, 30, Ephesians 6:20) While imprisoned, he had a number of supporters who stayed with him as "fellow prisoners" such as Aristarchus (4:10) and Epaphras (Philemon 23). These men were not actual prisoners, but apparently stayed voluntarily with Paul. This confinement lasted two years (Acts 28:30-31), yet few details are given about this time by Luke (the author of Acts as well as the gospel of Luke). We do know that during this time Paul wrote his 'prison letters': Ephesians (to the church at Ephesus), Philippians (to the church at Philippi), Colossians (to the church at Colossae), and Philemon (who was a friend of Paul's).

Based on the final letters of Paul – I Timothy, Titus, and 2nd Timothy, at the end of those two years, the apostle was released and went on to do further evangelical work. He preached for seven more year, perhaps going all the way to Spain (Romans 15:24) before being imprisoned again. The Bible does not tell us the exact time, date or manner in which he died although many traditions hold that he was beheaded by Nero.

"It was more important to Paul that he be a faithful minister than a free man."
(Wiersbe, 138)

"Ministers are servants to Christ, and fellow-servants to one another. They have one Lord, though they have different stations and powers for service. It is a great comfort under the troubles and difficulties of life, to have fellow Christians caring for us. Circumstances of life make no difference in the spiritual relation among sincere Christians; they partake of the same privileges, and are entitled to the same regards."
(Henry, 1440)

Great Quotes from Paul:

- "All Scripture is inspired by God and is useful to teach us what is true and to make us realize what is wrong in our lives. It corrects us when we are wrong and teaches us to do what is right. [17] God uses it to prepare and equip his people to do every good work" 2 Timothy 3:16-17
- "For there is one body and one Spirit, just as you have been called to one glorious hope for the future. [5] There is one Lord, one faith, one baptism, [6] one God and Father of all, who is over all, in all, and living through all." Ephesians 4:4-6
- "If I could speak all the languages of earth and of angels, but didn't love others, I would only be a noisy gong or a clanging cymbal. If I had the gift of prophecy, and if I understood all of God's secret plans and possessed all knowledge, and if I had such faith that I could move mountains, but didn't love others, I would be nothing. [3] If I gave everything I have to the poor and even sacrificed my body, I could boast about it; but if I didn't love others, I would have gained nothing. I Corinthians 13:1-3
- Love (try reading this and replacing "love" with your name!) is patient and kind. Love is not jealous or boastful or proud or rude. It does not demand its own way. It is not irritable, and it keeps no record of being wronged. [6] It does not rejoice about injustice but rejoices whenever the truth wins out. [7] Love never gives up, never loses faith, is always hopeful, and endures through every circumstance. I Corinthians 13:1-7
- "Rejoice in our confident hope. Be patient in trouble, and keep on praying." Romans 12:12
- "And I am convinced that nothing can ever separate us from God's love. Neither death nor life, neither angels nor demons, neither our fears for today nor our worries about tomorrow—not even the powers of hell can separate us from God's love. No power in the sky above or in the earth below—indeed, nothing in all creation will ever be able to separate us from the love of God that is revealed in Christ Jesus our Lord." Romans 8:38-39

QUESTION: Why do you think God allowed Paul to be imprisoned? Why does he allow hardships in any of our lives?

What are some of the images of Colossians 4?

An Open Door

"… that God would open to us a door for the word…" (4:3KJV)

Prayer Warriors

Devote yourselves to prayer… (4:2)
Pray for us… (4:3)
Pray that I will…" (4:4)

Think about this:

*What is the connotation of a wide open door?
*What other times has the image of a door been used in scripture? (Revelation 3:2, Genesis 4:7, Psalm 77:9, Matthew 7:7-8, I Corinthians 16:9)
*What aspects of your life do you hope for an 'open door'?

Think about this:

***Devote** – means to give or apply one's time, attention and self entirely to a particular activity, pursuit, cause or person.

*What type of life would one lead if one was devoted to prayer?

*How different would your life be if it was devoted to prayer?

WALKING IN PRAYER: How does this apply to me and my church?

Prayer

Devote yourselves to prayer… (4:2)

1. How big of a place does prayer have in your daily life?

2. How big of a place does prayer have in your church?

3. Do you regularly pray that God will give you opportunities to speak to others about Jesus Christ?

4. Does your church regularly pray that God will give opportunities to speak to others about Jesus Christ?

5. Does your church regularly pray for missionaries?

6. Do you regularly pray for missionaries?

7. What opportunities do you have in your daily life to speak to others about Jesus Christ?

Your Support System

(These people are gifts from God! Be Thankful!!!)

8. Do you have people who
    a. Spiritually encourage you?

    b. Spiritually educate you?

    c. Pray for you?

    d. Regular exhibit love, mercy and forgiveness?

    e. Give hospitality?

Appendix

Judaism

"The Lord said to Abram, 'Leave your country, your people and your father's household and go to the land I will show you. I will make you into a great nation and I will bless you; I will make your name great, and you will be a blessing. I will bless those who bless you, and whoever curses you I will curse; and all peoples on earth will be blessed through you.'"

Genesis 12:1-3

You shall have no other gods besides me.

You shall not worship any idol.

You shall not misuse God's name.

Remember the Sabbath day and keep it holy.

Honor your father and your mother.

You shall not murder.

You shall not commit adultery.

You shall not steal.

You shall not give false testimony.

You shall not covet anything that belongs to your neighbor.

The Ten Commandments

Exodus 20:1-17

About Spelling: I've done my best to be as accurate as possible, but in many instances, the spelling varied even within various Jewish texts and Internet site I referred to. (McG)

Key Person or Founder, Date, Location	❖ Abraham of the Bible, about 2000 B.C., in the Middle East. There are three main branches of Judaism, each with its own beliefs: Orthodox, Conservative, and Reform. (6)
Key Writings	Jewish ethics are derived from three basic sources of authority: (2) 1. **Torah:** The **Tanakh** (Old Testament), and especially the **Torah** (first five books of the Old Testament: Genesis, Exodus, Leviticus, Numbers, and Deuteronomy). (6) The will of God is described in the Torah. (Laws or "***mitzvot")*** This was the revelation of God to Moses. When the Jewish people were escaping from Egypt and were resting in the Sinai desert, Moses went up a mountain to pray and meditate upon god. There the Ten Commandments and other laws of God were revealed to him, later to be written down in the Torah (5) The Torah is handwritten in Hebrew and is on a scroll. (2) 2. **Talmud:**

	An explanation of the Tanakh. A long collection of writings and commentaries on Judaism by rabbis. The first section of the Talmud is termed the **Mishnah.** Another major part is termed the **Gemara.** Other parts of the Talmud are the **Halachah** and the **Agadah**. Although the Torah has scriptural authority in Judaism, nevertheless the interpretations of learned rabbis carry a great deal of respect. Their views were transmitted orally originally, but eventually they were committed to writing as the Talmud. It contains analyses and comments on such matters as the conduct of temple affairs and of religious ceremonies, on matters of hygiene, on questions of laws and their interpretation and on ethical issues. The Talmud also contains succinct sayings and short statements of wisdom on a variety of matters. These writings span a period of about 500 years from the first century A.D. to the fifth century A.D. Historically, two separate Talmuds were compiled. One is known as the **Palestinian** or **Jerusalem Talmud**, and the other as the **Babylonian Talmud**. Both are written in the same languages of Hebrew and Aramaic, but the Babylonian Talmud is longer. (5) The **Midrash** is an ancient commentary, explaining the meaning of the Talmud. (3) Each branch has it's own teachings: Orthodox, Conservative, and Reform. Writings of sages, such as **Maimonides** (see "Human Personalities"). (6) 3. **<u>Halakah:</u>** Meaning "path", it is a system of law regulating civil and criminal justice, family relationships, personal ethics and manners, social responsibilities, as well as worship and other religious observances. There are always new areas where the halakah is being considered, and it is frequent for the level of debate and argument to be vigorous in the Jewish community as a variety of viable interpretations are always available. (2) The Halachah encompasses Jewish law, both biblical and talmudic (oral), and includes the religio-judicial decisions handed down by great rabbinic scholars and commentators. The word itself literally means "the path" – referring to the laws Jews must follow if they are to abide by Jewish teaching. Those laws that emanate from the Bible are virtually unchangeable, while those deriving from the rabbis may, under given circumstances, be modified. Halachah covers nearly every conceivable event and activity, ranging from ritual and religious duties to ethical questions and including also civil and criminal law. (9)
Who is God?	❖ God is **spirit**. To Orthodox Jews, God is personal, all-powerful, **eternal** (no beginning no end), and compassionate. To other Jews, God is impersonal, unknowable, and defined in a number of ways. No Trinity. (6)
Who is Jesus?	Jesus is seen either as an extremist false messiah or a good but martyred Jewish **rabbi** (teacher). Many Jews do not consider Jesus at all. Jews (except Messianic Jews and Hebrew Christians – see "Denominations below) do not believe he was the Messiah, Son of God, or that he rose from the dead. Orthodox Jews believe the Messiah will restore the Jewish kingdom and eventually rule the earth. (6) The Jews still believe that the Messiah (the Anointed One) will come from the nation of Israel, from the tribe of Judah, and be a descendant of David. Isaiah 9:6 Old Testament prophecies about Jesus: (3) ❖ His birthplace – Micah 5:1-2 ❖ His birth by a virgin – Isaiah 7:14 ❖ Rejection by his own people – Isaiah 53:3 ❖ Betrayal by a close friend – Psalm 41:9

	❖ Events as he died – Psalms 22:14-18 ❖ The Messiah's sacrifice for his people – Isaiah 53:6 ❖ His resurrection from the dead – Psalms 16:10; 49:15
Who is the Holy Spirit?	Some believe the Holy Spirit is another name for God's activity on earth. Others say it is God's love or power. (6)
Prayer and Worship	❖ The **Synagogue** (means "bringing together" (2)) is the place where Jews gather for a variety of purposes including prayer. It should be remembered, however, that a great deal of Jewish devotion traditionally takes place in the home. The key place in the synagogue is arguably the **Ark.** It is in the Ark that the scrolls of the Torah are kept, often behind drawn curtains. The scrolls are wound around two wooden rods and kept in the Ark usually wrapped in velvet cloths. The **bimah** is the stand on which the Torah is read by the **cantor** or person who leads the prayers. A **rabbi** or teacher is the person who may preach a sermon from a pulpit discussing some aspect of the Torah. The Ark is usually kept at the eastern side of the synagogue, facing in the direction of Jerusalem. In a traditional synagogue there is a gallery around three sides of the building in which women and girls sit, and who are hence separate from the men who participate in the prayers and the service. (5) ❖ Orthodox male Jews when they pray wear religious dress that has great symbolism. The **Tallit** is a prayer shawl that is wound around the worshiper while he is reciting prayer, to show that god's law and commandments are wrapped around him. **Tefillin** are prayer phylacteries worn on the arm and head of a pray-er during **Shachrit**, the morning service. There are two kinds of tefillin: **tefillin shel yad** (for the hand) and **tefillin shel rosh** for the head).
What about sin?	Jews believe that man is not born good or evil; he is born free to choose between the two. (4)
How are you saved?	❖ Jews believe that anyone, Jew or Gentile, may gain salvation through commitment to the one true God and through moral living. (4) ❖ Some Jews believe that prayer, repentance, and obeying the Law are necessary for salvation. Others believe that salvation is the improvement of society. (6)
What happens after death?	❖ There will be a physical resurrection. The obedient will live forever with God, and the unrighteous will suffer. Some Jews do not believe in a conscious life after death. (6) ❖ Judaism believes in the human soul and its immortality, but no real comment is available on what life after death entails.
Important Holy Days	<u>**Sabbath or Shabbat:**</u> A holy day that begins on Friday evening at sunset, lasting until sunset on Saturday evening. (5) <u>**Rosh Hashanah: The New Year:**</u> The Jewish New Year begins in the autumn with the month of **Tishri.** It is a two day festival and a time to ask for forgiveness and prayers of repentance are made. A ram's horn **"shofar"** is blown in the synagogues, calling people to return to God, change their behavior, and be forgive. A meal follows in which bread and apples are dipped in honey to symbolize the hope for a sweet year ahead. It is believed that the heavenly Book of

	Life is opened and the good and evil deeds of each Jew are counted. (2) **<u>Yom Kippur: The Day of Atonement:</u>** Celebrated in early fall on Tishri 10 of the Jewish calendar, ten days after Rosh Hashanah, the New Year. It is marked by fasting, confession to God of sins committed during the last year, and prayers of forgiveness. Observance begins on Yom Kippur eve with the **"kol nidre"** service of repentance. Originally, Yom Kippur was the only day of the year when the high priest entered the inner sanctuary of the Temple (the Holy of Holies) to offer sacrifice. A goat – the so called scapegoat, symbolically carrying the sins of the Jewish people – was then driven into the desert. It is the holiest day in the liturgical year. It is a day of fasting for all fit adults. At they synagogue, the rabbi and may others wear white to symbolize purity. (2) **<u>Sukkoth: The Harvest Festival:</u>** Begins five days after Yom Kippur and lasts for seven days. Jews construct leafy booths (**"Sukkoth"**) in their gardens to commemorate the time when the people of Israel were instructed y God to build booths to live in when they were brought out of the land of Egypt. (Leviticus 23:42-43). Also called "**Tabernacles**". (2) **<u>Hanukkah: The Festival of Lights:</u>** Two months after Sukkoth on the 25th day of the month of **Kislev**. It lasts eight days and commemorates a miracle of God in 165 A.D. when a son of the priest Mattathias, a man called Judah, was given the name Judas Maccabbee (meaning "hammerer") because after three years of fighting he succeeded in defeating the Syrian Greek army. The temple had been seized and a statue of the Greek God Zeus had been installed. Maccabbee cleansed and purified the temple. Having only a single jar of holy oil to keep the eternal light before the ark burning for one day, it miraculously burned for eight days and nights. (2) **<u>Passover: Pesach</u>** Remembers the deliverance of the Israelites from Egyptian slavery. (2) **<u>Purim:</u>** Commemorates the story of Esther in the bible. (2) **<u>Shavuot: The Feast of Weeks:</u>** Celebrates the giving of the Ten commandments at Mt. Sinai. (2)
Policies Towards Women/ **Gender Concepts**	In the Mishnah and the Talmud, discussions about women are numerous and deal with the legal status of women in both the public and private aspects of life. (2) ❖ The Talmud says that husbands should regard wives as equal, to be honored and supported. The Talmud is concise: "If your wife is short, bend down to listen to her advice." (2) ❖ There is severe criticism of women in the Talmud derived from the second creation story in the book of Genesis, in which woman is made from the rib of man and she disobeys God by eating the fruit of the tree of the knowledge of Good and Evil. This story contrasts with the first creation narrative in Genesis 1, in which men and women are created equal. The rabbis' commentary on this includes the view that Adam had two wives, the first Eve, who the call Lilith, and the second Eve, who ate the fruit in Genesis 2. The commentary sees Lilith arguing with her husband that she is equal, but she uttered God's name and was therefore changed into demon form to haunt humanity; she caused

	the serpent to tempt the other Eve in the Garden of Eden. God punished her for this and made her subservient to men. (2) ❖ Men and women suffered the same fate for adultery or apostasy, but women were still seen as lesser in status. A woman had no right to divorce, and lineage was passed down through the patriarchal line in biblical times. There are stories of influential matriarchs, e.g. Sarah, Rebekah, Leah, and Rachel. Deborah's leadership as a judge of Israel is also notable. (2) It should be noted that a formal Jewish divorce is known as a **get,** and is a formal text in which the woman is granted freedom to marry again. Furthermore, civil divorce does not constitute the end of a Jewish marriage until the formal get has been obtained properly and delivered. (Internet: http://www.ahavat-israel.com/ahavat/torat/divorce.asp) ❖ In strict Orthodox Judaism, women and men have traditionally had clearly defined and very separate roles. Women are superior in the home, in teaching their children, and in preparing for Shabbat and other festivals. Men have total supremacy in the public domain, i.e. in religious life, in synagogues, and in courts. (2) In America, Orthodox rabbis allow women to conduct their own services, which includes reading from the Torah, but they may not undertake those duties on behalf of men. In Great Britain, women are not allowed to conduct their own services on the premises of a synagogue, but only privately in a home. (2) ❖ Reform Judaism has accepted women rabbis and abolished partition. Progressive Judaism believes in the equality of men and women so that women can fully participate at every level of synagogue leadership and worship. (2)
Terminology and Definitions	**Covenant: *(b'rit)*** a special kind of agreement between God and the Jews. Essentially a covenant is an agreement, both religious and moral, which places certain obligations upon the Jews, and which also stipulates certain consequences if the agreement is not kept. (5) ❖ Covenant between God and Abraham: In the book of Genesis God promises Abraham that he will have many descendants, among whom will be kings and rulers of people. This covenant promised by God is declared by Him to be an everlasting covenant. The covenant between God and Abraham was to be marked by the act of circumcision of all males. (5) ❖ Covenant between God and Moses: In the book of Exodus God promises Moses that if the Israelites abide by the covenant, then they will be held by God in the highest esteem, above all other people. The terms of His covenant are strict monotheism, as well as the remainder of the Ten Commandments. (5) Diaspora: The word comes from the Greek meaning dispersion, and normally refers to the phenomenon of the many Jewish communities living around the world away from Israel. The notion of diaspora started in 586 BC when the Babylonians, having overcome the Kingdom of Judah, forcible removed many Jews to Babylonia to work as slave labor. Although this would have been an extremely difficult period for the Jewish captives, they succeeded in maintaining their own culture and religion. Synagogues were built as a focus for religious practice. (5) Decalogue: another name for the Ten Commandments (3) Minyan: Jewish prayer is ordinarily a group activity done with a quorum of 10 people called a minyan. A complete formal prayer service cannot be conducted without a quorum

	of at least 10 adult Jewish men; that is, at least 10 people who are obligated to fulfill the commandment to recite the prayers. This prayer quorum is referred to as a minyan (from a Hebrew root meaning to count or to number). Certain prayers and religious activities cannot be performed without a minyan. This need for a minyan has often helped to keep the Jewish community together in isolated areas. (Internet: http://www.jewfaq.org/prayer.htm#Group)
Other Beliefs or Practices	❖ The Jews believe that the **purpose of life** is summed up in love for God and love for one's neighbor. Deuteronomy 6:5, Leviticus 19:18. This love is based on the love God has for his people. The way to express love for God and one's neighbor is set out in the Ten Commandments. (3) ❖ **Kosher:** Everything in Judaism is concerned with ethics and right moral action. All the ritual is intended to guide better behavior. The dietary laws illustrate the way that the religious, the ritual, and the ethical coincide in the faith. There are three main aspects of keeping kosher: (2) **1.** Only certain species are permitted for eating: cows, sheep, chicken, and fish; others are forbidden : pigs, shellfish. (2) **2.** The slaughter of animals must be done in a certain way to minimize pain. (The Torah includes a way against slaughtering a calf in the presence of its mother.) (2) **3.** There is no mixing of meat and dairy products at a meal. (2) ❖ **Jerusalem** is considered to be the holy city. (6) The most holy locations include the Temple Mount and the Western or Wailing Wall. In 1005 BC King David established rule over the city, and his son Solomon built the first temple in 969 BC. In 586 BC Nebuchadnezzar, the king of Babylon destroyed Jerusalem and many Jews were exiled to Babylon. The dome of the Rock is the Jerusalem mosque, constructed in 691 AD. It is built on the same rock as the Temple of Jerusalem. (5) ❖ **Yarmulke** (Yiddish) or **kipah** (Hebrew)**:** a head covering custom dating back a few thousand years. It is not a formal obligation. Young Jewish men seen today wearing small skullcaps do so because of religious convictions or to demonstrate their allegiance to the Jewish community. (9) ❖ **Circumcision** - the **Bris Milah ,** *Bris* means covenant, *milah* means to cut. Preformed on the 8th day, The kabbalistic writings teach us that seven days represent the physical world of creation. Thus, when a child has lived for eight days, he has transcended the physical to the metaphysical. The covenant joining body and soul, physical and spiritual, can now take place. A bris has no meaning when performed before the eighth day. The Bris has two parts, the actual circumcision and the naming. Circumcision is the surgical removal of the foreskin from the penis. (Internet: http://www.torahview.com/bris/html/the_bris.html)

Branches/ **Denomination/Number of Adherents**	There are approximately 5 ¾ million Jews, divided roughly as follows among the major denominations ❖ 1 million Reform Jews ❖ 1 ¼ million Conservative ❖ 1 ½ million Orthodox. ❖ The others are not affiliated with a religious institution, although many belong to secular Jewish organizations. (9)
Differences within denominations	*Some comparative differences of Orthodox, Reform, and Conservative Judaism are found in the table following the bibliography. (McG)*
Important Symbols and Their Meanings	The name **Star of David**, derived from the Hebrew "Magen David" (literally "Shield of David"), hints that there would be a direct connection between the star and (King) David. A legend states that David would have worn a Star of David on his shield, whenever he went into battle Not a single shred of evidence was ever found for this however. According to the Encyclopedia Britannica, the symbol--which historically was not limited to use by Jews--originated in antiquity, when, side by side with the five-pointed star, it served as a magical sign or as a decoration. In the Middle Ages the Star of David appeared with greater frequency among Jews but did not assume any special Jewish religious significance; it is found as well on some Christian medieval cathedrals. The Magen David gained popularity as a symbol of Judaism when it was adopted as the emblem of the Zionist movement in 1897, but the symbol continued to be controversial for many years afterward. When the modern state of Israel was founded, there was much debate over whether this symbol should be used on the flag. It now appears on synagogues, Jewish tombstones, and the flag of the State of Israel. (Off the Internet)
Human Personalities Worth Noting	**Moses Maimonides** (1135-1204) was the foremost intellectual figure of medieval Judaism. He is famous for three works: his commentary on the Mishnah, his code of Jewish law, and his "Guide of the Perplexed." He was born into an educated family, who left Spain for Morocco because of the persecution of the Jews of Cordoba by a fanatical Islamic sect. There Maimonides began to study medicine, but his family fled again due to persecution and moved to Palestine. They finally settled in the 1160s near Cairo in Egypt, where he eventually became the court physician for Sultan Saladin and his family. He was also a lecturer, a doctor with his own practice, and a leader of the Jewish community. His writings are vast. (2)

Scientology

Scientology: Scio (Latin) know, logos (Greek) the word or outward form by which the inward thought is expressed and made known. Thus, Scientology means knowing about knowing. (15)

For the first time there exists a proven, workable technology to improve the functions of the mind and rehabilitate the potential of the spirit. This is auditing. (15)

Key Scriptures:

- **Matthew 7:15** Beware of false prophets who come disguised as harmless sheep but are really vicious wolves.

Key Person or Founder, Date, Location	L. Ron Hubbard (1911-1986). Founded 1954 in California. Current headquarters in Los Angeles, California (6) The first Scientology church was incorporated in December 1953 in Camden, New Jersey, by American science fiction author[8][9] L. Ron Hubbard. The church has been the subject of much controversy. Its world headquarters are located in the Gold Base, unincorporated Riverside County, California. David Miscavige is Scientology's leader since Hubbards death in 1986. Headquarters are in Clearwater, Florida. (16) **Scientology:** comes from the Latin *scio*, which means "know" and the Greek word *logos*, meaning "the word or outward form by which the inward thought is expressed and made known." Thus, Scientology means knowing about knowing. Scientology is an applied religious philosophy developed by L. Ron Hubbard. It is the study and handling of the spirit in relationship to itself, universes and other life. (15)
Key Writings	*Dianetics: The Modern Science of Mental Health* and others by Hubbard. *The Way to Happiness* (6) **Dianetics:** comes from the Greek words *dia*, meaning "through" and *nous*, meaning "soul." Dianetics is a methodology developed by L. Ron Hubbard which can help alleviate unwanted sensations and emotions, irrational fears and psychosomatic illnesses. It is most accurately described as *what the soul is doing to the body through the mind.* (15)
Purpose	To "clear" the planet and free Thetans (eternal spirits in bondage to matter). (11) Official Aims of Scientology: A civilization without insanity, without criminals and without war, where the able can prosper and honest beings can have rights, and where man is free to rise to greater heights. (16)
Who is God?	Does not define God or Supreme Being, but rejects biblical descriptions of God. Everyone is a "thetan", an immortal spirit with unlimited powers over its own universe, but not all are aware of this. (6) What the Church refers to as "the Supreme Being" Is purposely left undefined and does not become particularly relevant in Scientology theory or practice. It is variously implied to be or

	referred to as "nature," "infinity," "the Eighty Dynamic," "all Theta" (life) and so forth. Usually the individual Scientologist is free to interpret this, God in whatever manner he wishes. (11)
Who is Jesus?	Jesus is rarely mentioned in Scientology. Jesus was not the Creator, and not an "operating thetan: (in control of supernatural powers, cleared from mental defects). Did not die for sins. (6) Jesus is a man who was not particularly enlightened whom the church invented as the savior of the world. Some Scientologists may classify Him as an "Operating Thetan" (OT): a person aware of his true nature and abilities. (11)
Who is the Holy Spirit?	The Holy Spirit is not part of this belief. (6)
Human Authority here on earth	**auditing:** Scientology counseling, taken from the Latin word *audire* which means "to hear or listen." Auditing is a very unique form of personal counseling which helps an individual look at his own existence and improves his ability to confront what he is and where he is. **Auditing by List:** a technique used in certain auditing procedures. **auditor:** a minister or minister-in-training of the Church of Scientology. *Auditor* means one who listens, from the Latin *audire* meaning "to hear or listen." An auditor is a person trained and qualified in applying auditing to individuals for their betterment. An auditor does not do anything *to* a preclear, he works together with the preclear to help the preclear defeat his reactive mind. (15)
Beliefs or Practices	Man in his true nature is an eternal spirit being with divine powers. (AKA a Thetan) (11) All humans are made up of a body, mind, and "thetan, " that is their essential immortal spirit. (16) Members observe the birth of Hubbard and anniversary of publication of *Dianetics.* Controversy follows the group worldwide. *Time* magazine and *Reader's Digest* have published damaging exposes. Various media have reported that church leaders have had indictments and/or convictions for burglary, wiretapping, conspiracy, and other felonies. 1. Self (the urge to survive as an individual) 2. Creativity (the urge to survive through family). 3. Group survival (the urge to survive through a group such as a nation, team, community, race, etc.) 4. Species (the urge to survive through the survival of the human species) 5. Life forms (the urge for life itself) 6. Physical universe (the urge of the universe to survive) 7. Spiritual dynamic (the urge for the survival of the life source) 8. Infinity (the urge to exist as infinity or God) (14) Reincarnation (14) **Sea Org:** The core of every great religion in history has been a group of individuals dedicated to achieving the goals of the religion. In Scientology, these individuals are part of a fraternal religious order known as the Sea Organization, or Sea Org. While relatively few in number, its members play a crucial role in virtually every aspect of the ministry and expansion of Scientology. And, like their counterparts in other faiths, Sea Organization members occupy the most essential and trusted positions in the senior churches in the Scientology ecclesiastical hierarchy. (15)

	assessment: an auditing technique which helps to isolate specific areas or subjects on which a preclear has charge so that they can be addressed in auditing. (15)
Prayer and Worship	Scientology Churches Scientology churches are open daily, and they hold weekly services. These meetings do not include prayer and do not make reference to God. Clergy perform christenings, baptismal rites, weddings, and funerals. (16)
What about sin?	No sin or need to repent. One must work with an "auditor" on his "engrams" (hang-ups) to achieve the state of ":clear," then progress up the "bridge to total freedom." (6) Falsehood or ignorance and especially that which opposes Scientology is the closest the church comes to claiming something to be a "sin". Satan is a Christian myth; redefined to include Scientology concepts. (11) (See accompanying chart: Scientology 101)
How are you saved?	Salvation is freedom from reincarnation. (6)
What happens after death?	Hell is a myth. (6) People who get clear of engrams become operating thetans. (6) Death is an inconsequential dropping of the body which all Thetans have experienced trillions of times. (11) Heaven and Hell are both Christian myths, or mental implants from previous lives. (11) Individuals continue up the Operating Thetan Bridge until one is free from the cycle of birth and death and from the restraints of matter, energy, space, and time; this "eighth dynamic" is the urge toward existence as infinity, or the Supreme Being. (16)
Important Holy Days	March 13 - Hubbard's birthday (in 1911) May 9 - publication of *Dianetics* (in 1950) 2nd Sunday in September - Auditor's Day October 7 - annual meeting of International Association of Scientologists (14) National Founding Day: February 8 L. Ron Hubbard's birthday - March 13 *Dianetics* publications anniversary - May 9 Sea Or Day - August 12 (celebrates the Sea Organization, a group of devout Scientology recruits Clear Day - Sept 4 - to commemorate the 1965 inauguration of the Clearing Course Auditor's Day - 2nd Sunday in September - to honor those dedicated to "brining man up the Bridge to Total Freedom" Freedom Day - December 30 - to celebrate the official recognition of the Church of Scientology in the United States (16)

Branches/ Denominations/Number of Adherents	77,000 (adherents.com) or "millions" (official Scientology figures) (14)
Human Personalities Worth Noting	**Current Scientologists (and deceased famous people who were in Scientology when the passed away):** • **L. Ron Hubbard** - best-selling science fiction author; founder of Scientology • John Travolta - actor • Chick Corea - influential American jazz pianist and composer • Brandy (Norwood) - R&B singer, actress • Tom Cruise - actor, movie star • Kirstie Alley - actress • Mimi Rogers - actress (2nd generation) • Anne Archer - actress • Jennifer Aspen - actress • Catherine Bell - actress • Jenna Elfman - actress • Juliette Lewis - actress • Priscilla Presley - actress • Karen Black - actress • Kelly Preston - actress • Lisa Marie Presley - singer; daughter of Elvis Presley • Edgar Winter - musician • Chaka Khan - singer • Sonny Bono - singer ("Sonny and Cher"), U.S. Representative • Mary Bono - widow of Sonny Bono; U.S. Representative http://www.adherents.com/largecom/fam_scientologist.html
Countries where popular	Banned: Germany, France, Wikipedia, Russia Because Scientology has multiple membership "levels" (attending a lecture, going for an "auditing session," and so forth), it is difficult to know exactly how many adherents the church has. One online source lists 4,200 groups, missions, and churches worldwide, serving some ten million Scientologist (www.Religioustolerance.org). (16)

Jehovah's Witness

"You are my witnesses," declares the Lord. *Isaiah 43:10*

Its aggressive brand of proselytizing has made the Jehovah's Witnesses one of the most successful religious cults in this century. (11)

Jehovah's Witnesses are usually better drilled about their beliefs than Christians are. (3)

Key Scriptures:

- 144,000 going to heaven: Revelations 7:4 And I heard how many were marked with the seal of God—144,000 were sealed from all the tribes of Israel:
- No Blood Transfusions: Acts 15:29 You must abstain from eating food offered to idols, from consuming blood or the meat of strangled animals, and from sexual immorality. If you do this, you will do well. Farewell.
- No Hell: Matthew 25:46 "And they will go away into eternal punishment, but the righteous will go into eternal life."
- Salvation Through Works: Ephesians 2:8-9 God saved you by his grace when you believed. And you can't take credit for this; it is a gift from God. [9] Salvation is not a reward for the good things we have done, so none of us can boast about it.

What Was The Cultural Climate of the Day That Caused the Formation of Jehovah's Witnesses?

The Millerite (Adventist) Movement of the nineteenth century was largely responsible for what has been called the Great Second Advent Awakening. William Miller (1782-1849) was originally a deist (a person who believes that God created the universe, but has not been actively involved since). After two years of study, Miller converted to Christianity and became a Baptist lay leader, convinced that the Bible contained coded information about the end of the world and the second coming of Jesus.

In 1831, Miller began to preach and write articles attracting thousands of followers with his message – based on prophecies in Daniel and Revelation – that the return of Christ would occur sometime between two spring equinoxes: March 21, 1843, and March 21, 1844. The end did not happen. Samuel Snow, a Millerite, then interpreted the tarrying time referred to in Habakkuk 2:3 as equal to seven months and ten days, delaying the end time to October 22, 1844. Followers sold their properties and possessions to be ready for the event, although the well-known story of them sitting on their rooftops in ascension robes has no historical foundation. That prophecy also did not come to pass. Many believers left the movement or regrouped in what has become known as The Great Disappointment. Miller died in 1849 without supporting or endorsing any of the various groups. His followers called themselves Adventists; the group was often referred to as Millerites by others.

Jehovah's Witnesses are Millennialists and believe in the literal return of Christ and inauguration of his kingdom on earth. The group arose late following the Great Disappointment that came after the failure of William Miller's prophecies in 1831 that the world would end with the advent of Christ in 1834. The return of Christ was also expected in 1920, 1925, 1940, 1975, and 1984.

Key Vocabulary	**Millenialists –** belief in the literal return of Christ and his earthly kingdom which will exist for a 1000 years. REVELATIONS 20:1-7 **Jehovah** – God, one person, not part of a trinity, Jesus was the first thing that Jehovah created. **Witnesses** – members of the sect known as Jehovah's Witnesses **Anointed Class** – select group of 144,000 Jehovah's witnesses who will be born again and go to heaven. REVELATIONS 7:4 **Second Class** – all those other faithful Witnesses who will not be born again, will not go to heaven, but will live on "paradise earth" forever. REVELATIONS 21:1 **Exclusivism –** No other organization on earth operates or disseminates to God's will nor has the true interpretation of the Bible. **Watchtower Bible and Tract Society –** publication arm of Jehovah's Witness **Proselytizing** – Going door to door to win others to the faith. **Kingdom Hall** – Meeting place of Jehovah's Witnesses **Lord's Evening Meal** – once a year "communion" in which only anointed class may partake
Key Person or Founder, Date, Location	Charles Taze Russell (1852-1916). At Russell's death, Joseph F. Rutherford became president. (6) Known as Russellites" until 1931. (3) Began 1879 in Pennsylvania. (6) Headquarters in Brooklyn, New York. (6)
Key Writings	All current Watchtower publications including the bible (New World Translation only), Reasoning from the Scriptures, You Can Live Forever in paradise on Earth, Watchtower and Awake! magazines. (6) The Jehovah's Witnesses' interpretation of Christianity and their reject of the orthodoxy influenced them to produce their own translation of the Bible. Although this work claims to be a translation, the Witnesses have yet to prove its reliability. Many biblical scholars regard it as a poor and inaccurate translation and see it as worded to give biblical support to the group's own doctrines. For example, in John 1:1 the Divine Logos (Christ) is reduced in nature and status: "In the beginning…and the Word was a god." The normative Greek translation is, "In the beginning was the Word and the Word was with God, and the Word was God." (2)
Purpose	To declare the name and coming of the Kingdom of Jehovah God. (11)
Who is God?	One –person God, called Jehovah. No Trinity. Jesus is the first thing Jehovah created. (6)
Who is Jesus?	Jesus is not God. Before he lived on earth, he was Michael, the archangel. Jehovah made the universe through him. On earth he was a man who lived a perfect life. After dying on a stake (not a cross), he was resurrected as a spirit; his body was destroyed. Jesus is not coming again; he "returned" invisibly in 1914 in spirit. Very soon, he and the angels will destroy all non-Jehovah's Witnesses. (6) Jesus is "a god" but not "the God. (3) Jesus "was and is and always will be beneath Jehovah" and that "Christ and God are not coequal". (3)

Who is the Holy Spirit?	Impersonal "holy spirit" is not God, but rather an invisible, active force from Jehovah. (6)
Human Authority here on earth	• Charles Taze Russell (led: 1872-1916) (6) • Joseph Franklin Rutherford (led: 1917-1942) (3) • Nathan Homer Knorr (led: 1942-1977) (3) • Frederick W. Franz (led: 1977-1992) (3) • Milton G. Henschel (led: 1992-) (3)
Beliefs or Practices	One cannot fully understand Watchtower Society literature unless one understands that there are two distinct classes of believers within the Witnesses. Without realizing who a given section of literature is referring to, one may become confused; for example, by assuming that terms like "anointed class" refer to all Jehovah's Witnesses when in fact they do not. (11) The Anointed Class vs. The Second Class: These are the 144,000 specific Jehovah's Witnesses (God's elect), and only they are "born again." (SEE REVELATIONS 7:4)This class is explained by the Witness theory that since 33 A.D. Jehovah has been choosing 144,000 individuals as a special class of people to rule with Him in heaven. No one in Old Testament times can be apart of this class, since before Christ no one could be "born again." The 144,000 have different responsibilities, a different way of salvation and a different destiny than the "second" class of individuals, which are the "other sheep," the vast majority of Jehovah's Witnesses. While they will one day rule in heaven with their elder brother Jesus, they now rule the "other sheep" here on earth, seeing themselves in a servant role. It appears that virtually all of the 144,000 have already been selected, so that among the millions of Witnesses the average person today has virtually no expectation of being the elect. A few may express the "hope" of election, and this seems to be determined by personal conviction. Thus the vast majority of Witnesses have no desire to be 'born again," and they do not expect, or intend, to go to heaven. They expect to live on a "paradise earth" forever, assuming they pass the many future divine tests required of them. (11) Exclusivism: Claim to represent the only organization on earth through which Jehovah God operates and disseminates His will; to supply the true interpretation of the Bible. "We belong to NO earthy organization… We adhere only to that heavenly organization… All the saints now living, or that have lived during this age, belonged to OUR CHURCH ORGANIZATION: such are all ONE Church, and there is NO OTHER recognized by the Lord. Hence any earthly organization which in the least interferes with this union of saints is contrary to the teachings of Scripture and opposed to the Lord's will. (The Watchtower, March 1, 1979, p. 16, Emphasis in original) (11) Known as the Watchtower Bible and Tract Society. (6) Russell founded the Herald of the Morning in 1879 which developed into today's Watchtower magazine. From an initial monthly print run of 4,000 copies it now prints 18 million copies every month in more than 100 languages. It has become the most influential way of perpetuating the Jehovah's Witness teachings. (3) Active members encouraged to distribute literature door-to-door. (6) All Jehovah's Witnesses are strongly encouraged to be very active in proselytizing for the movement. Most Jehovah's Witnesses are expected to spend five hours a week at training sessions held in a kingdom hall, as well as door to door visiting in a selected area. Often, a Jehovah's Witness will devote up to 100 hours a month to the movement. (3) Seven Steps that Jehovah's Witnesses use to win others to their faith: (3) 1. Put Jehovah's Witness literature into the hands of a prospective convert.

	2. Revisit this person to establish further personal contact. 3. Introduce the person to the study of Jehovah's Witness books. 4. Encourage the person to attend teaching meetings at a kingdom hall. 5. Encourage the person to attend services at a kingdom hall. 6. Encourage the person to become active in "publishing" – giving out Jehovah's Witness tracts. 7. Encourage the person to become baptized by immersion in a kingdom hall. **Do not** • observe holidays or birthdays • vote • salute the flag work in the military, Jehovah's Witnesses refuse to fight in times of war, not from strict beliefs that killing is wrong (because God allowed it in the Old Testament) but on the grounds of the invalidity of taking up arms for an earthly power or government. (2) • accept blood transfusions. (6) Jehovah's Witnesses in modern society are known for their refusal to accept blood transfusions. This act is based on Jewish law in the bible about taking blood into the body through mouth or veins, which violates God's laws (Gen 9:4, Lev. 17:14, Acts 15:28-29). Their views on organ transplants and vaccinations have changed several times during the recent past but now seems to have settled as being a matter for the believer's individual conscience. (2) • sing the Star Spangled Banner. (3) Believe Armageddon will occur soon. (6) The cross should not be used as a symbol. (3) Jehovah's Witnesses are Millennialists (belief in a future one thousand year reign of Christ)and believe in the literal return of Christ and the inauguration of his kingdom on earth. (2)
Prayer and Worship	Meet on Sunday's in "Kingdom Halls." (6) Once a year, Lord's Evening Meal; only "anointed" ones may partake.
What about sin?	A weak view of sin is held. (11)
How are you saved?	Be baptized as Jehovah's Witnesses. Most followers must earn everlasting life on earth by "door-to-door work." Salvation in heaven is limited to 144,000 "anointed ones." This number is already reached. (6) Jehovah's Witnesses teach that there is no salvation outside their own ranks. (3) By faith and works. Man is capable of achieving salvation without spiritual rebirth. (11)
What happens after death?	In the end, there are three basic possibilities for the future state after death: 1. Recreation as a spirit in heaven (immortality as one of the 144,000 elect. 144,000 live as spirits in heaven. The rest of the righteous, "the great crowd," live on earth, and must obey God perfectly for 1000 or be annihilated. (6)

	2. Recreation to a probationary general future physical life on earth for a 1000 years. 3. Depending upon the outcome of this life and its testings there will result either eternal life upon earth or extinction forever. (11) Death brings annihilation – temporary for those "resurrected" (recreated) to life, eternal for the wicked. (11) Hell: • Heaven is a place reserved for only the 144,000 "elect"; the idea of an eternal hell is a "doctrine of demons." (11) • The Watchtower denies the existence of hell as a place of everlasting punishment for the wicked. They argue, "The doctrine of a burning hell where the wicked are tortured eternally after death cannot be true mainly for four reasons: 1. It is wholly unscriptural; 2. It is unreasonable; 3. It is contrary to God's love; and 4. It is repugnant to justice." (Let God Be True, p. 9) (1)
Important Holy Days	Do not observe holidays or birthdays. (3)
Policies Towards Women/ Gender Concepts	Affirmation: Jesus taught equality; no discrimination in serving. MEN are Head of Household and Women are to submit; complement husband. They embrace Proverbs 31.
Branches/ Denominations/Number of Adherents	Under Nathan Homer Knorr's leadership (Rutherford died in 1942), the membership rose from just over 100,000 to two and a quarter million. (3)
Differences within denominations	There are some 24+ sects of the Jehovah's Witnesses. These sects retain the heretical teachings of Charles Russell in spite of sounding Christian. Here are a few: • Layman's Home Missionary Movement of Chester Springs, PA (50,000-100,000 members). • Dawn Bible Students Associate of East Rutherford, NJ (20,000-40,000 members). • The Associate Bible Students and the pastoral Bible Institute. Also known as Berean Bible Institute • Back to the Bible Way • The Christian Believers • The New Creation Bible Student's Association (11)

Mormon

AKA "The Church of Jesus Christ of Latter-day Saints"

TRUE OR FALSE?

1. There are multiple worlds and multiple Gods.
2. God has a wife and lives on a planet near the star Kolob.
3. God and Adam are one in the same.
4. God is in charge of this earth ONLY.
5. The Garden of Eden is in Independence, Missouri.
6. Mary was one of God's many wives and she was impregnated through a sexual union with God which then created Jehovah – AKA Jesus.
7. People can evolve into gods and goddesses.
8. Goddesses will spend eternity in full submission to their god-husbands and will give birth forever.
9. Satan is Jesus' brother.
10. Just about every single Mormon goes to heaven.
11. The Mormon Church has assets over 1 billion dollars and are the largest land owners in the US.
12. All of the important documents pertinent to the Mormon faith are written on gold plates.
13. A stand-in can get baptized for you and guarantee your salvation.
14. The LDS Church was the first in post-biblical times to include Jesus' name in the official name of the church instead of using the name of a reformer, a practice, or an event.

ANSWERS:

1. **There are multiple worlds and multiple Gods.**

   TRUE. Mormons believe that God created multiple worlds and each world has people living on it. They also believe that multiple Gods exist but each has their own universe. We are only subject to our God and if we obtain the highest level of heaven we can become gods ourselves.

2. **God AKA ELOHIM has a wife and lives on a planet near the star Kolob.**

   TRUE. *Pearl of Great Price, Abraham 3:2-4, 9; J of D, 26:214.* God the Father was once a man, but became God. He has a physical body, as does his wife (Heavenly Mother). They live on a planet near the great star Kolob.

3. **God/Elohim and Adam are one in the same.**

   TRUE He is (in early Mormonism) Adam who fell in the Garden of Eden

4. **God AKA Elohim AKA Adam is in charge of this earth ONLY.**

   TRUE As an infinite number of gods and earths exist, God the Father of Jesus Christ is creator and ruler of this earth only.

5. The Garden of Eden is in Independence, Missouri.

TRUE. *Doctrine and Covenants 116; Journal of Discourses, 10:235*; Smith named the Spring Hill, Daviess County, Missouri area Adam-Ondi-Ahman. The Garden of Eden, was relocated, according to Mormonism, in what is now Independence, Missouri. (11)

6. Mary was one of God's many wives and she was impregnated through a sexual union with God/Elohim/Adam which then created Jehovah – AKA Jesus.

TRUE *Journal of Discourses 8: 116; J of D 8: 211; J of D 8: 115; Mormon Doctrine p.546-547.* "Jehovah" of the Old Testament; the first begotten spirit child of Elohim ("God the Father"), who "created" (or fashioned) him by physical sexual union with Mary, one of his wives. (11)

7. Men can evolve into gods.

TRUE. Man is an eternal refashioned spirit intelligence having the innate capacity to evolve into godhood. *Journal of Discourses 1:50-51; J of D 8:115; Doctrine and Covenants Section 132:20*

8. Goddesses will spend eternity in full submission to their god-husbands and will give birth forever.

TRUE. Doctrine and Covenants 84:33-9; Goddesses are always subject to a god. Women are denied the Priesthood (meaning they are denied authority-not the same as Catholic priesthood). "In the LDS universe, theologically described as the real eternal universe, each man who achieves the highest degree of the Celestial Kingdom is worth many times more than each woman, even the women who qualify at that highest Celestial level, because each man who achieves Godhood-level may have numerous God-wives, but each God-wife may have only one husband. This can only mean that each "heavenly father" is worth many times more than each "heavenly mother." And, even if the ratio were strictly one to one, the male God, not the female God, holds the priesthood authority and is the only one of the God parents to whom his earth-mortality children are allowed to pray. LDS Apostle Orson Pratt wrote, "Each father and mother will be in the condition to multiply forever and ever" (The Seer, 37)

9. Satan is Jesus' brother.

TRUE. *Journal of Discourses 8: 116; J of D 8: 211; J of D 8: 115; Mormon Doctrine p.546-547.* Satan is one of the innumerable preexistent spirits created by Elohim and his wife; hence the spirit brother of all men and women, including Christ Himself. Because of his primeval rebellion, he was not permitted to inherit a body as the rest of his brothers and sisters. In essence, Satan and demons once represented potential men and women but are now consigned to live as spirits forever.

10. Just about every single Mormon goes to heaven.

TRUE. All other salvation is considered "damnation," which to Mormons does include participation in various degrees of glory. Mormonism is almost universalistic, teaching that all will be saved except a very few "sons of perdition." Some Mormons teach that even these will be saved. (11)

11. The Mormon church has assets over 1 billion dollars and are the largest land owners in the US.

TRUE. The Mormon church has an investment portfolio of bonds and stocks worth more than one billion dollars. It controls more than 100 businesses which generate more than four hundred million dollars a year. It owns property in all of the states of America and has become the nation's largest private landowner. There are 46,000 Mormon missionaries active throughout the world. They aim to have 100,000 missionaries by the year 2000.

12. All of the important documents pertinent to the Mormon faith are written on gold plates.

TRUE. The Book of Mormon was written by many ancient prophets by the spirit of prophecy and revelation and their words were written on gold plates. These gold plates were given to Joseph Smith and eleven other witnesses have seen these gold plates for themselves. Their testimony is also provided in the current Book of Mormon. (14)

13. **A stand-in can get baptized for you and guarantee your salvation.**

TRUE. The practice of proxy baptisms or "baptism for the dead" attempt to help nonchurch members make it into heaven by allowing devout members of LDS serve as "stand-ins" at continuous baptismal ceremonies held in Mormon temples.

14. **The LDS Church was the first in post-biblical times to include Jesus' name in the official name of the church instead of using the name of a reformer, a practice, or an event.** TRUE

Mormon

AKA "The Church of Jesus Christ of Latter-day Saints"

What! Are Christians ignorant? Yes, as ignorant of the things of God as the brute beast.

Journal of Discourses, 6:25 (11)

Key Scriptures:

- One God: Isaiah 43:10 There is no other God - there never has been, and there never will be.
- God's Nature: Numbers 23:19 God is not a man, so he does not lie. He is not human so he does not change his mind.
- God's Existence: Psalm 32:2 Your throne, O LORD, has stood from time immemorial. You yourself are from the everlasting past.

Key Person or Founder, Date, Location	**Mormon** – prophet/historian who quoted and abridged the words of the numerous ancient prophets and written on gold plates. He gave his translation to his son, **Morni** (AD 421) who added a few more things to his father's writing and hid the gold plates in the hill Cumorah. Then on September 21, 1823 in a glorified, resurrected state, Morni appeared to Prophet Joseph Smith and instructed him relative to the ancient record and its destined translation into the English language. Eventually, Joseph Smith was given the gold plates and through the gift and power of God was able to translate them.(14) **Joseph Smith, Jr.** (1805-1844), founded the Church of Jesus Christ of the Latter-day Saints in 1830 in new York. Headquarters in Salt Lake City, Utah. (6) Joseph Smith, Jr. was born on December 23, 1805, in Sharon, Vermont. Smith was the fourth of ten children of Joseph and Lucy Mack Smith. In 1817, the family moved to Palmyra, New York (near present-day Rochester). Most of the members of the Smith family soon joined the Presbyterian church, but young Joseph remained undecided. His argument was that all the strife and tension among the various denominations made him question which denomination was right. It was this conflict that set the stage for Joseph's alleged first vision. (1) Although the Mormon church began to grow in numbers while expanding westward, it was not without persecution. While in prison for ordering the destruction of a local paper for publishing anti Mormon material, Smith and his brother Hyrum, were shot and killed by an angry mob of

	about 200 people. (1) Brigham Young took over after Smith's death. He settled the group at Salt Lake Valley in Utah. By the time of his death in 1877, the membership was approximately 150,000. (1) **Brigham Young** – (1801-1877) Second president and successor to Joseph Smith, Jr. Led the Mormons westward to Salt Lake City, Utah, where the church is still headquartered. (1) **Ezra Taft Benson** – (1899-1994) former US Secretary of Agriculture under President Eisenhower and thirteenth president of the LDS. **Living Prophets:** In Mormonism, the current president of the Mormon church supposedly has the ability to receive divine revelations and is considered a "living prophet." His revelations are considered superior to all past revelations. (1)
Key Writings	*The Book of Mormon; Doctrine and Covenants; Pearl of Great Price,* the Bible (King James Version only or Smith's "Inspired Version"); authoritative teachings of Mormon prophets and other LDS "general authorities" (6) The Book of Mormon was written by many ancient prophets by the spirit of prophecy and revelation and their words were written on gold plates. These gold plates were given to Joseph Smith and eleven other witnesses have seen these gold plates for themselves. Their testimony is also provided in the current Book of Mormon. (14) Within the book of Mormon are four kinds of metal record plates: The Plates of Nephi, The plates of Mormon, The Plates of Ether, and the Plates of Brass. (14) Believe that the Bible as the Word of God must be translated correctly. Wherever it disagrees with Mormon theology, it is considered incorrect due to textual corruption or false translation or interpretation. (11) "The Book of Mormon is the most correct of any book on earth, and the keystone of our religion, and a man would get nearer to God by abiding by its precepts, than by any other book." (Joseph Smith) (14)
Connections	*The Seven Habits for Highly Effective People*, By Stephen Covey and the Power-Glide Language Courses created by BYU professor Dr. Robert Blair. Covey explains in his book, *The Divine Center*, that he has discovered how to communicate Mormon truths to non-Mormons by simply changing his vocabulary. He writes, "I have found in speaking to various non-LDS groups in different cultures that we can teach and testify of many gospel (LDS) principles if we are careful in selecting words which carry out meaning but come from their experience and frame of mind." (11, *Divine Center, p. 240)*
Purpose	To evangelize the world with the message of Jesus Christ as interpreted by Joseph Smith and the Mormon church; to baptize the dead for their salvation; for individual members to strive to attain godhood on the basis of personal righteousness and merit. (11)
Who is God?	God the Father was once a man, but became God. He has a physical body, as does his wife (**Heavenly Mother**). No Trinity. Father, Son, and Holy Ghost are three separate gods. Worthy men may one day become gods themselves. (6) God is an exalted physical man; "**Elohim**" of Old Testament; a deity "created" (technically, "fashioned") by the sexual union of his divine mother and father. As an infinite number of gods and earths exist, God the Father of Jesus Christ is creator and ruler of this earth only. He is (in early Mormonism) Adam who fell in the Garden of Eden, which was then relocated, according to Mormonism, in what is now Independence, Missouri. (11)

	• A physical body of flesh and bones (vs. spirit) • Mortal and finite (vs. immortal and infinite) • Changeable and evolving (vs. immutable, never changing) • Physically localized (vs. omnipresent) • Polygamous and/or incestuous (vs. Jesus was monogamous, celibate) • Exalted saved man (vs. eternal deity) • Has a feminine counterpart, the Heavenly Mother (vs. no feminine counterpart) • At one time, in early Mormonism, was considered to be Adam (vs. Adam, a creation of God) (11)
Who is Jesus?	Jesus is a separate god from the Father (Elohim). He was created as a spirit child by the Father and Mother in heaven, and is the "elder brother" of all men and spirit beings. His body was created through sexual union between Elohim and Mary. Jesus was married. His death on the cross does not provide full atonement for all sin, but does provide everyone with resurrection. (6) "Jehovah" of the Old Testament; the first begotten spirit child of Elohim ("God the Father"), who "created" (or fashioned) him by physical sexual union with Mary, one of his wives. (11) • A created being, elder brother of Lucifer (vs. uncreated God) • Common, one of many gods (vs. unique and of supreme importance throughout time, eternity and all creation) • Conceived by a physical sex act between God the Father (Adam or Elohim) and Mary, thus NOT through a true virgin birth • Once sinful and imperfect (vs. eternally sinless and perfect) • Earned his own salvation (vs. as God, never required salvation) • A married polygamist (vs. an unmarried monogamist) (11)
Who is the Holy Spirit?	The "holy spirit" is not God, but is an influence or electricity-like emanation from God (also called the "light of Christ"). (6) The Holy Ghost is a man with a spiritual body of matter. (11)
Who is Man?	An eternal refashioned spirit intelligence having the innate capacity to evolve into godhood. Men on earth were first created as spirit offspring of Elohim and his wife through physical sexual intercourse. Thus, men are created or fashioned as preexistent spirits and subsequently inhabit the products of human sexual intercourse (a physical body) in order to attempt to gain exaltation or godhood. (11)
Human Authority here on earth	The living prophet's word is a source of authority. The present-day living prophet is Ezra Taft Benson. His title is President of the Council of the Twelve Apostles. In a speech on February 26, 1980 he said that the living prophet (head of the church) is "more vital to us than the standard works." (1)

Beliefs or Practices	• The leader of the church (aka Prophet or President) is the mouth-piece of the Lord and delivers messages from Him. • No infant baptism. Children are baptized at the age of eight. • Tithe 10% • **No** alcohol, tobacco, coffee, or tea. • **Baptism** on behalf of the dead. • Two-year **missionary commitment** encouraged. • **Door-to-door** proselytizing. • **Secret temple rituals** available only to members in good standing. • Extensive **social network**. • People of **African ancestry** not granted full access to Mormon priesthood and privileges until 1978. (6) • Historically and at present **necromantic (contacts** with the dead) and spiritualistic revelations and other contacts; development of psychic powers interpreted as gifts of the Holy Spirit. (11) • "It should be stressed that any claims by Mormon leaders and writers concerning official Mormon history, early doctrine, apologetics and so on are generally not to be trusted. The Mormon Church has engaged in a **protracted whitewashing of its early history and doctrines**. As a result, most Mormons are unaware that previous divinely inspired teachings may contradict official Mormon doctrine today. " (11) • In regard to the **Second Coming of Christ**, the Mormons speak of the Second coming of the earth god Jesus, but they have also referred to the Second Coming of the god Joseph Smith (11, *Journal of Discourses, 7:289; 5:19)* • The **Fall of Adam and Eve** was ultimately beneficial; predestined by Elohim for the spiritual progress and ultimate welfare of all mankind. (11) • Against **homosexuality**. • **Sex** outside of marriage is forbidden. • No **stimulants** of any kind. • **Vegetarianism** is encouraged but not mandatory. (2) • The Mormons officially practiced **polygamy** until 1890. Due to increasing enforcement of a federal law against polygamy, which included fines and imprisonment, Wilford Woodruff, fourth president/prophet, rescinded polygamy as a practice *but not as a doctrine) out of practical necessity. Government pressure threatened the very existence of all Mormon temples, and polygamy had been a chief reason Utah had been denied statehood at least six times. (2) • Mormons tend to view **financial prosperity** as a sign of God's blessing. Their corporate wealth confirms their belief that Mormonism is wealthy because it is pleasing to God, and tithing is a principle means of church income. (11) • **Proxy baptisms** - The practice of proxy baptisms or "baptism for the dead" attempt to help nonchurch members make it into heaven by allowing devout members of LDS serve as "stand-ins" at continuous baptismal ceremonies held in Mormon temples.(15)

	• **LDS congregations** assemble each Sunday and typically meet for a hour. Buildings are small, modest "chapel" buildings. Visitors are always welcome. There is no firm and fixed liturgy but typically these gatherings include congregational hymns and prayer, the partaking of the sacrament (communion), and two or three short messages from assigned speakers (laymen in positions of leadership as there are no paid clergy). Various Sunday school cases are also commonly offered either before or after the sacrament meeting. (15) • The building of **Temples** is emphasized and currently there are more than 100 in the world. In these holy places, LDS church members learn Mormon doctrine and engage in Mormon ordinances (marriage, baptism, proxy baptism). Only LDS church members in good standing may participate in temple rituals. (15) • **Holidays** they celebrate are Easter, Christmas, Anniversary of the Founding of the Mormon Church (April 6), John the Baptist's visitation of Joseph Smith (May 15th), Pioneer Day commemorates the 1847 arrival of the first group of LDS settlers to Salt Lake Valley (July 24) and General conference (first weekends in April and October). (15)
What about sin?	Mormonism holds a less than biblically orthodox view of sin in that is scriptural content is downplayed in some way. First, the Mormon concept of works-salvation teaches that good works cancel the penalty of sin. Second, is teachings give the Fall a positive role in fostering spiritual growth and maturity. (11)
What about Satan and demons?	Satan is one of the innumerable preexistent spirits created by Elohim and his wife; hence the spirit brother of all men and women, including Christ Himself. Because of his primeval rebellion, he was not permitted to inherit a body as the rest of his brothers and sisters. In essence, Satan and demons once represented potential men and women but are now consigned to live as spirits forever. (11)
How are you saved?	Resurrected by grace but saved (exalted to godhood) by works, including faithfulness to church leaders, Mormon baptism, tithing, ordination, marriage, and secret temple rituals. No eternal life without Mormon membership. (6) True salvation in Mormonism is achieved by personal merit and effort with the goal of attaining "exaltation," or godhood, in the highest part of the celestial kingdom. There one may participate in "eternal increase"; that is, as a god one may beget (or fashion) innumerable spirit children just as Elohim has. All other salvation is considered "damnation," which to Mormons does include participation in various degrees of glory. Mormonism is almost universalistic, teaching that all will be saved except a very few "sons of perdition." Some Mormons teach that even these will be saved. (11) Believes that there were two great civilizations. One came from Jerusalem in 600 B.C., and afterward separated into two nations, known as the Nephites and the Lamanites. The other came much earlier when the Lord confounded the tongues at the Tower of Babel. This group is known as the Jaredites. After thousands of years, all were destroyed except the Lamanites, and they are the principal ancestors of the American Indians. The book of Mormon is the person ministry of the Lord Jesus Christ among the Nephites soon after his resurrection. It puts for the doctrines of the gospel, outlines the plan of salvation, and tells men what they must do to gain peace in this life and eternal salvation in the life to come. (14)

What happens after death?	Eventually nearly everyone goes to one of three separate heavenly "kingdoms," with some achieving godhood. Apostates and murderers go to "outer darkness." (6) **Celestial Heaven** – highest of the three heavens in Mormon teaching. (1) **Terrestrial Kingdom** – a secondary degree of glory (heaven) reserved for those who, though honorable, failed to comply with the requirements of exaltation to Godhood. (1) **Telestial Kingdom** – lowest division of glory (heaven) in Mormonism, reserved for those having no belief in Christ or the gospel. (1)
Policies Towards Women/ **Gender Concepts**	Brigham Young advocated the death penalty for any White mixing blood with a "Negro"(4) In 1978 the president of the Church claimed a new revelation that admitted blacks to the priesthood, although women are still excluded from the priesthood. The church provides strong opposition to the Equal Rights Amendment, believing that the effects would prove disruptive to family life. (2) By the time they are teenagers, the Saints begin assuming adult responsibilities and gender roles. All worthy males are eligible for "ordination" to the almost entirely lay (nonprofessional) priesthood. At about twelve years of age, young men who are obedient to religious and community standards usually are "ordained" to the office of "deacon" (the first round of the lesser or 'Aaronic Priesthood"). Continued conformity usually results in subsequent ordinations to the successive offices of "teacher" and "priest" in the Aaronic Priesthood at approximately two-year intervals. At about age eighteen (or high school graduation), worth young men usually are ordained to the office of 'elder" in the "high) "Melchizedek Priesthood." Adult males who have demonstrated religious commitment may be ordained to the last regular office of "High Priest." (3) LDS women are not ordained to the priesthood. They instead have primary responsibility for the care, socialization, and teaching of young children (in Sunday school and otherwise), much of the work associated with the church's extensive social calendar, many aspects of the operations of the Saints' extensive welfare programs (such as canning and preparing food as well as providing clothing), assisting and supporting the priesthood (as with teaching and sharing the gospel), and many other activities traditionally associated with the roles of wife and mother. LDS women begin assuming some of these responsibility and roles as teenagers. At age twenty-one, women may serve on a mission at home or abroad, although missions primarily are a priesthood responsibility and far fewer young women than men take advantage of serving on a mission. (3)
Branches/ **Denominations /** **Number of Adherents**	Today the church has over four million members worldwide. (1) There are nearly 9 million Mormons in the world – over half of whom live in America. (3) The Mormon church has an investment portfolio of bonds and stocks worth more than one billion dollars. It controls more than 100 businesses which general more than four hundred million dollars a year. It owns property in all of the states of America and has become the nation's largest private landowner. There are 46,000 Mormon missionaries active throughout the world. They aim to have 100,000 missionaries by the year 2000. (3) Not all Mormons followed Young west. A significant minority, headed by Smith's wife Emma and his son Joseph III, remained in Missouri and Illinois and formed the Reorganized church of Jesus Christ of Latter Day Saints, headquartered today in Independence, Missouri. Many other Mormon splinter groups also survived, and some still exist. (4)

Christian Science Church

The Church of Christ Science

The First Church of Christ, Scientist

"The Healing Truth dawned upon my sense, and the result was that I rose, dressed myself, and ever after was in better health than I had before enjoyed." Mary Baker Eddy (2)

Christian Science is neither Christian nor scientific because every important doctrine of historic Christianity is rejected by CS. The claim of divine revelation by Mrs. Eddy is contradicted by the facts that clearly attest she does not represent the God of the Bible. Although she speaks in the name of Jesus, her teachings conflict with His in every respect." (1)

Key Scriptures:

- Faith Healing: **John 4:43-51**
- Reality: 2 Corinthians 4:18 **For what is seen is temporary, but what is unseen is eternal.**

Key Person or Founder, Date, Location	Mary Baker Eddy (1821-1910) Founded 1875 in Massachusetts. Current headquarters in Boston, MA (6)  Phineas Quimby - was a self-professed healer who applied hypnosis and the power of suggestion in affecting his cures. He called his word, "The science of the Christ" and "Christian Science." Mrs. Eddy became an enthusiastic follower of Quimby in 1862 after her back injury was healed by him. She wrote letters to the Portland (Maine) Even Courier praising Quimby and comparing him to Jesus Christ. (1) LINES ON THE DEATH OF DR. P.P. QUIMBY, WHO HEALED WITH THE TRUTH THAT CHRIST TAUGHT, IN CONTRADISTINCTION TO ALL ISMS. Did sackcloth clothe the sun, and day grow night, All matter mourn the hour with dewy eyes, When Truth, receding from our mortal sight, Had paid to error her last sacrifice? Can we forget the power that gave us life? Shall we forget the wisdom of its way? Then ask me not, amid this mortal strife, -- This keenest pang of animated clay, -- To mourn him less: to mourn him more were just, If to his memory 'twere a tribute given

	For every solemn, sacred, earnest trust, Delivered to us he rose to heaven. Heaven but the happiness of that calm soul, Growing in stature in the thrown of God: Rest should reward him who hath made us whole, Seeking, through tremblers, where his footsteps trod. ....MARY M. PATTERSON (LYNN, FEB 22, 1866) http://marybakereddy.wwwhubs.com/ A few weeks after Quimby's death, Mrs. Eddy fell over on a sidewalk and struck her back on the ice, and was taken up for dead. She came to consciousness amid a storm of vapors from cologne, chloroform, ether, camphor, etc., to find herself the helpless cripple she was before she saw Dr. Quimby. Feeling that she had not long to live, she asked for her Bible, and whilst reading an account of one of Jesus' healings, she felt God's presence very strongly and shortly afterwards rose from her sick bed. "The physician attending said I had taken the last step I ever should, but in two days I got out of bed alone and will walk; but yet I confess I am frightened . . . I think that I could help another in my condition if they had not placed their intelligence in matter. This I have not done, and yet I am slowly failing." writes Mrs. Eddy in a letter to Mr. Julius Dresser, a fellow patient that was healed by Quimby. In the same letter she asked Mr. Dresser whether he could help her overcome the present physical difficulties caused by her accident, as she believed that he could and was best fitted to take up where Quimby left off. Mr. Dresser did not respond to this appeal, and Mrs. Eddy had to depend on her own interpretation of Quimby's method. She recovered her health, however, and marked this period as the time that she came to fully understand the "Science of Christianity," which she named Christian Science—A term that had been used by Dr. Quimby on at least one occasion. http://marybakereddy.wwwhubs.com/ Eventually, Eddy attempted to separate any connection between herself and Quimby when charges of borrowing his ideas surfaced. However, the facts are otherwise. "As far as though is concerned, Science and Health is practically all Quimby." (Earnest Sutherland Bates & John V. Dittermore, ary Baker Edy: The Turth and The Tradition, 1932, p. 156) (1)
Key Writings	*Science & Health, With Key to the Scriptures;* *"I should blush to write of* Science and Health with Key to the Scriptures *as I have, were it of human origin and I apart from God its author, but as I was only a scribe echoing the harmonies of Heave in divine metaphysics, I cannot be super-modest of the Christian Science Textbook." (Eddy, Christian Science Journal, Jan. 1901) (1)* *Miscellaneous Writings; Manual of the Mother Church*, and other books by Mrs. Edy. The Bible (not as reliable). *Christian Science Journal, Christian Science, Sentinel,* and other writings. (6) Christian Science, like many other cults, claims further revelations that goes "beyond the Bible" that is to say, new divine truth previously unrevealed. (1) "Your dual and impersonal pastor, the Bible, and Science and Health with Key to the Scriptures, is with you; and the Life these give, the Truth they illustrate, the Love they demonstrate, is the great Shepherd that feedeth my flock, and leadeth them 'beside the still waters.'" Eddy (14)
Purpose	The concern of the modern church is for ethical thinking and high moral standards, as well as devotion to God and a central and abiding commitment to the healing ministry. Health and happiness are restored not by going to doctors or mental health specialists but by applying to all of life attitudes in line with the already existing divine harmony. For the Christian Scientist, both sickness and sin are the result of error. (2)

Who is God?	God is an impersonal Principle of life, truth, love, intelligence, and spirit. God is all that truly exists (matter is an illusion). (6)
Who is Jesus?	Jesus was not the Christ, but a man who displayed the Christ idea. ("Christ" means perfection, not a person.) Jesus was not God, and God can never become man or flesh. He did not suffer and could not suffer for sins. He did not die on the cross. He was not resurrected physically. He will not literally come back. (6)
Who is the Holy Spirit?	Holy spirit is defined as the teaching of Christian Science. Impersonal power. (6)
Human Authority here on earth	*Mrs. Eddy passed away December 3, 1910. Today there is a self-perpetuating board of directors which governs the church. (1)* *The Church of Christ, Scientist and its officers are governed by the By-Laws in the Church Manual. Church officers officially appointed by The Christian Science Board of Directors include a President, Clerk, Treasurer, and two Readers at The Mother Church. The Board also appoints members of the Board of Education (Christian Science teachers), the Board of Lectureship (public speakers), and military chaplains. Other church roles which are not appointed by the Board include Christian Science practitioners, Christian Science nurses, and volunteer chaplains at correctional facilities. Global Christian Science churches and societies appoint their own officers, readers, Sunday School teachers, Reading Room librarians, etc. Everyone shares the same pastor, the Bible and Science and Health. http://christianscience.com*
Beliefs or Practices	• Members use Christian Science practitioners instead of doctors. Healing comes from realizing one cannot be sick or hurt and that the body cannot be ill, suffer pain, or die (matter is an illusion). (6) • Attracts followers by claims of miraculous healing. (6) • CS does not believe in the most basic scientific thought, that the universe is physical and is subject to natural laws. It teaches that the material world does not exist and that the spirit is the only reality. So the physical world and human body are mere illusions. From this it follows that the body cannot be ill, suffer pain, or die. (14) • CS "services", which are lectures in halls, can appear to be Christian, because the Bible is read. But there are no sermons, only selected readings from Eddy's books which she claimed was co-authored by God. (14)
Prayer and Worship	Christian Science services include hymns, prayers, and warm fellowship. Also, instead of ministers giving personal sermons, democratically elected laypeople read quotes or "readings" from our "pastor," which is the Bible and *Science and Health with Key to the Scriptures* by Mary Baker Eddy. Every church around the world will feature similar readings on Sundays. They may also simultaneously offer classes for Sunday School students under the age of 20. At Wednesday testimony meetings, the readings are unique from one church to the next, and participants are invited to spontaneously share gratitude and testimonies of healing. http://christianscience.com
What about sin?	In CS there exists no evil. "Matter and evil (including all inharmony, sin, disease, death) are unreal" (1) "Evil is a false belief, God is not its author." (1)

How are you saved?	Humanity is already eternally saved. Sin, evil, sickness, and death are not real. (6) As evil is an illusion, the idea of the death of Christ on the cross for our sins is unnecessary. "The material blood of Jesus was no more efficacious to cleanse from sin when it was shed upon "the accursed tree" than when it was flowing in his veins as he went daily about his Father's business." (1)
What happens after death?	Death is not real. Heaven and hell are states of mind. The way to reach heaven is by attaining harmony (oneness with God). (6)
Terminology and Definitions	• *Animal magnetism - evil wrong thinking, which causes an individual to experience the illusion of evil. Malicious animal magnetism can kill those it is practiced against. (1)* • *At-one-ment - it is the unity between the mind of God and the mind of man as demonstrated by Christ. (1)* • Christian Science Journal - *periodical of CS, used for recruitment of new members. (1)* • Christian Science Monitor - *Newpaper published by CS, highly regarded in the secular world with little religious propaganda. (1)* • Christian Science Sentinel - *periodical of CS, used for recruitment of new members. (1)* • *Immortal Mind - God in CS theology. (1)* • *Quimby, P.P. - early 19th century mesmerist and psychi healer from whom Eddy learned the principles she later claimed were revealed from God as CS (1)* • Science and Health with Key to the Scriptures - *Contains the teachers of Eddy. The book is regarded as a revelation with more authority than the Bible (1)*
Branches/ Denominations /Number of Adherents	There is no way to get an accurate number of Christian Scientists today since the Church Manual says, "Christian Scientists shall not report for publication the number of members of the Mother Church, nor that of the branch Churches." (1) Observers estimate worldwide membership at 420,000. (1) 1 million members, 3,000 churches in 56 countries with 700,000 members in the USA (14)
Differences within denominations	CS is nonaggressive in recruiting new members, who are free to enter and leave the movement. (2)

Islam

TRUE Statements About Islam!

1. ***Adam, Noah, Abraham, Moses, Jonah and Jesus are all great prophets of Islam.***

Belief in prophets The Qur'an lists 28 prophets of Allah. These include Adam, Noah, Abraham, Moses, David Jonah and Jesus. To the Muslim, the last and greatest prophet is Mohammed. (4)

Ashura: Holiday held by Shi'ite Muslims on the tenth day of the first month to commemorate Husair, who was the Prophet's grandson who died in battle. For Sunnis, the celebration remembers the birth of Adam, the saving of Noah, and the Exodus of the Jews. (2)

2. ***Muslims recognize the Torah, Psalms and the Gospel of Jesus as revealed scriptures.***

Biblical Law of Moses, Psalms, and Gospel of Jesus (the Injil) accepted by Qur'an, but considered by Muslims to be "corrupted". (6) These revelations include the Torah (of Moses), the Suhuf (books of the prophets), Zabur (psalms of David), Injil (gospel of Jesus). The Qur'an supercedes all other revelations and is the only one of which we still have the original text. All of the others have been corrupted, almost beyond recognition. (1)

- **Belief in revealed scripture** There are four: The Torah of Moses, The Psalms of David (Zabur), the Gospel of Jesus (Injil), and the Qur'an. Only the Qur'an is uncorrupted. (4)

3. ***Every Muslim must make at least one trip to Mecca in his or her lifetime to gain salvation.***

Make pilgrimage to Mecca (once in a lifetime). Pilgrimage=Hajj It is expected of all Muslims at least once in their lifetimes. It can be extremely arduous on the old or infirm, so in their cases they may send someone in their places. The trip is an essential part in Muslims' gaining salvation. It involves a set of ceremonies and rituals. (1)

4. ***Islam is the fastest growing world religion.***

Islam is the fastest growing world religion. In 1900 there were 200,000,000 Muslims. In 1950 there were 370,000,000 Muslims. In 2000, there will be 1,340,000,000 Muslims. Over six million Muslims live in America. (3)

5. ***Islam brought about major positive changes for women.***

Pre Islam	Post Islam
Marriage arrangements so loose as to be scarcely recognizable	Sanctified marriage making it the sole lawful locus of the sexual act
Women were like any other possession. (2)	
Daughters had no inheritance rights	Daughters receive half portions of the sons
Birth of a daughter regarded as a calamity, often killed	Infanticide forbidden
	Leaves open the possibility of education, suffrage and vocation
	Koran requires that a woman give her free consent before she may be wed
	Mohammad countenanced divorce only as a last resort.

	Woman provided with a sum of money which she retains in its entirety should a divorce ensue.
	Women are not the source of sin. Rather Adam and Eve are both equally to blame. (2)

6. ***Islam has proved fertile ground for almost every antiwoman custom it has encountered.***

The most urgent and relevant task is to examine the way the faith has proved such fertile ground for almost every antiwomen custom it encountered in its great march out of Arabia. When it found veils and seclusion in Persia, it absorbed them; when it found genital mutilations in Egypt, it absorbed them; when it found societies in which women had never had a voice in public affairs, its own traditions of lively women's participation withered. (pp. 231-232)

7. ***Muslims are circumcised.***
8. ***Muslims don't drink alcohol.***
9. ***Muslims don't gamble.***

Other practices include circumcision, abstention from alcohol, gambling and certain foods. (1)

10. ***Jesus is mentioned almost four times more often then Muhammad in the Qur'an (the Muslim holy book).***

Jesus is mentioned 97 times in the Qur'an, while Muhammad is mentioned only 25 times. (3)

11. ***Muslims believe that Jesus was born of a virgin and was sinless. He is called the Messiah.***

The Muslim view of Jesus is significant. The Qur'an presents Jesus as one of the great prophets. He is called the Messiah. He is declared to have been born of the virgin Mary. He lived a sinless life (Surah 19:19). He accomplished many wonderful miracles. He is going to return to earth again to establish Islam throughout the earth. He is called "the Word of God" (3:45) and "the Spirit from God" (4:171). But they are adamant in declaring that Jesus is not the Son of God and Savior. In fact, they believe that equating anyone with God is blasphemy, the unforgivable sin. They do not believe that he was crucified. Instead, God took him to heaven without dying, and someone else died in his place. (1)

12. ***Muslims believe in angels, a day of judgment, and one God.***

Belief in angels The chief angel is Gabriel, who is said to have appeared to Mohammed. There is also a fallen angel named Shaitan (from the Hebrew "Satan") as well as the followers of Shaitan, the jinns (demons). (4)

Belief in one God The doctrine of predestination. The belief that no one can change what He has decreed. From this doctrine comes the most common Islamic phrase, "If it is Allah's will." (4)

Belief in a day of judgment On the "last day," the dead will be resurrected. Allah will be the judge, and each person will be sent to heaven or hell. Heaven is a place of sensual pleasure. Hell is for those who oppose Allah and his prophet Mohammed. (4)

13. **Muslims believe in confession, prayer, tithing, and fasting.**

❖ Confess that Allah is the one true God and that Muhammad is his prophet. Profession of Faith=Shahada Creed=Kalima No matter what country they live in, all Muslims share certain basic beliefs and practices. When a Muslim pronounces these words of belief, he or she formally becomes a member of the Muslim community. (12)

❖ Pray five times daily facing Mecca. Prayer=Salat Upon Rising, at noon, in midafternoon, after sunset, and before retiring. The worshipper must recite the prescribed prayers in Arabic while facing the K'aba in Mecca. (1)

❖ Give alms (money). Almsgiving=Zakat Alms originally were voluntary, but all Muslims are legally required to give 1/40 of their income for the destitute. (1)

14. Islam means submission.

Islam means "submission" (3)

15. There are two main branches of Islam: Sunni and Shi'ite. They share a same central core of beliefs and practices but differ over who has the authority to interpret the Islamic religious law.

Shiite is a minority branch of Islam that had broken with the mainstream in the years following the prophet Muhammad's death. The majority of the early Muslims agreed that their leader should be appointed by consensus of the elders, as was the long tradition of the desert. Since the Arabic word for "tradition" is sunnah, them became known as the Sunni Muslims. A minority, however, felt that Muhammad's successor should come from within his own family, and chose his son-in-law and cousin, Ali. They were the Shiat Ali, or partisans of Ali, known today as Shiites. Because of their origins as dissenters, Shiites hold it an obligation to question those in power, and revolt against them if necessary. And because their origins lay in the defeat of Ali and his sons, Shiites' most profound identification is with the beaten and poor. (pp.16-17)

While Sunni Muslims assume a direct relationship between believers and God, Shiites believe in the mediation of a highly trained clergy. Usually, each Shiite chooses a high-ranking clerical thinker and follows any religious ruling, or fatwa, from that person. For those who chose Khomeini, it meant that they ordered every detail of their life according to the opinions he set out in his eighteen volumes of religious interpretation. "Some ayatollans – literally, reflection of God. In Shiite Islam, the most learned of religious teachers and law interpreters receive this title – say women must wear gloves but Khomeini said that the lower part of the hand could be uncovered. Other ayatollahs considered the female voice arousing and barred women from speaking in mixed gatherings unless the first put a stone in their mouths to distort the sound. Khomeini had no problems with the female speaking voice. (pp.25-26)

Sunnis and Shi'ites share the same central beliefs and practices, but differ over the issue of who can interpret the Islamic religious law. Following the death of Muhammad, disagreement arose as to the necessary qualifications and exact function of his successors as leaders (Imams) of the Muslim community.

Shi'ites: those who insist that only members of the Prophet's clan, specifically, the descendants of Muhammad's daughter Fatima and her husband 'Ali, could qualify to interpret Islamic religious law. Shi'ism has three major subdivisions as well as numerous offshoots. The majority are called Twelvers (Ithna Ashariyya), because they recognize twelve Imams beginning with 'Ali; the twelfth disappeared in 873 but will return as the Mahdi (messiah). (2)

Sunnis: believe that successors should be appointed by community consensus. (2)

16. There are more Sunnis Muslims than Shi'ite Muslim.

The majority of Muslims (85%) are **Sunnis** and a substantial minority (15%) are Shi'ites.

17. Proper prayer follows a rigorous routine of timing, cleanliness, posture and attitude with absolutely NO EXCEPTIONS.

You cannot perform prayer if you are unclean and impure. Muslims, therefore, perform ritual cleansing. This act includes a system of ablution, which contains rich symbolic meaning. The intention of this cleansing is to purify body and soul and can be rendered invalid by deep sleep, unconsciousness, or bodily discharges. (2)

Four postures in prayer are always followed: standing, bowing, prostration, or sitting. The pray-er must have clean clothes and be in a clean place, and with the right intentions towards God. (2).

18. Hamas is a radical Islamic group that calls for war to the death against Israel.

Hamas is the Islamic group that calls for a war to the death against Israel. (p. 153) The Hamas devotes two articles of its thirty-six article charter to the role of Muslim women. Women, it says, "manufacture men and play a great role in guiding and educating the [new] generation. The enemies have understood that role, and therefore they realize if they can guide and educate [the women] in a way that would distance them from Islam, they would have won that war. ....Therefore, we must pay attention to the schools and curriculi upon which Muslim girls are educated, so as to make them righteous mothers, who are conscious of their duties in the war of liberation..." (p. 154)

19. In its ideal form, the Islamic state isn't a nation.

In its ideal form, the Islamic state isn't a nation in any modern sense of the word. It has no borders. It would be a political and religious union of all Muslims, modeled on the community Muhammad set up in medina. There would be no political parties, just a single, unified Islamic ummah, or community. At its head would be a caliph, literally, successor, who would follow in the footsteps of the prophet Muhammad as the Muslims' leading political and religious authority. (p. 189)

20. Mohammad was a sensualist who extolled the right for women to have sexual pleasure, never required a woman to wear a veil or seclude herself and who's first wife, Khadijah supported him financially for their entire marriage.

There is an immense body of hadith in which Muhammad and his closest disciples extol women's sexuality and their right to sexual pleasure. (p. 38)

At the age of 25 he married a wealthy 40-year-old widow name Khadijah. "He was a poet rather than a theologian; a master improvisor rather than a systematic thinker. That he was in the main simple in his tastes and kindly in his disposition there can be no doubt; he was generous, resolute, genial and astute: a shrewd judge and a born leader of men. He could, however, be cruel and vindictive to his enemies; he could stoop to assassination; and he was undeniable sensual" (Anderson, 1) Muhammad had his first vision by the age of 40. At first he was unsure of the source of these visions, whether divine or demonic. His wife, Khadijah, encouraged him to believe they had come from God. Later she became his first convert. (1)

Khadija, Muhammad's first wife and the first Muslim woman, was never required to veil or seclude herself, and never lived to hear the word of God proclaim that 'Men are in charge of women, because God has made the one of them to excel the other, and because they spend of their property [to support them]." Such a revelation would have come strangely from Muhammad's lips had Khadija still been alive and paying his bills (as she did for their entire marriage). (p.4)

Muhammad's first wife, Khadija, died in 619 A.D.when he was 49 years old. He was heartbroken. He married Sawda, a widowed older woman … Aisha a beautiful child of his best friend, Abu Bakr who she was only six, the marriage wasn't consummated immediately, and she remained with her family for a number of years … Hafsah, the twenty-year-old daughter of his close friend Omar; an older woman, Zeinab, whose generosity earned her the name "Mother of the Poor," and who died just eight months later; and Umm Salamah, a famous beauty whose arrival caused Aisha the first pangs of the jealousy that would blight the rest of her life. (pp. 78-79) … he married five additional women including two Jews and a Coptic Christian. (There is a difference of opinion about whether he married all three of these women or simply kept one or two of them as concubines.) (p. 86)

Muhammad's increasing number of divine revelations on women seemed more and more influenced by the need to achieve tranquility in his own household. Aisha, for one, wasn't afraid to point out the coincidence. "It seems to me," she said tartly, "your Lord makes haste to satisfy your desires." (p. 83)

Jealousy, fighting, and nagging caused Muhammad to withdraw from the harem and keep to himself for almost a month. He returned from his retreat and offered each of his wives a divinely inspired ultimatum: they could divorce him and have a rich settlement of worldly goods, or they could stay with him, on God's terms, which included never marrying again after his death. In return, they would be known forever as Mothers of the Believers, and reap a rich reward in heaven. All the women chose to stay. (p. 86)

When Muhammad died, he spent his last weeks with his beloved Aisha – the other wives having given up their turns to allow him to spend his last weeks with her. When he died she was just 19. A lonely future stretched before her: childless, and banned from remarriage. All she had left was influence. Because she had spent so much time at Muhammad's side, she became a leading religious authority. Originally, 2,210 hadith (additions to the Koran) were attributed to her: ninth century scholars, dismissing the word of a mere woman, threw out all but 174. (p. 87)

There is no God but Allah, and Muhammad is the Prophet of Allah.

The Kalima (Creed)

In the name of the One God, the Compassionate One, the Merciful.

Praise be to God, the Lord of the Universe-

The Compassionate One, the Merciful –

The Ruler on the Day of Judgment.

We worship you and from you we seek help.

Guide us into the straight path –

The path of those to whom you have shown mercy –

Not those who have incurred your anger, nor those who go astray.

From the beginning of the Qur'an,

known as "The Opening".

A devout Muslim repeats this prayer five times a day. (3)

ISLAM

Key Scriptures

- Genesis 21:12 But God told Abraham, "Do not be upset over the boy and your servant. Do whatever Sarah tells you, for Isaac is the son through whom your descendants will be counted. [13] But I will also make a nation of the descendants of Hagar's son because he is your son, too.
- Hagar & Ishmael's Story: Genesis 16, Genesis 21:8-21, Genesis 25:12-18, Galatians 4:23-25

"Islam"

"Islam" is not a proper noun, but a way of living, a way of practicing peace. Islam was the name ascribed to the doer of Salam (Muslim). To be a Muslim means therefore to be gathered together as the universal people of Allah, a people who radically submit in peace to the absolute oneness of God. (13)

The word "Islam" is derived from the root s-l-m, with the connotation of "peace" but the secondary sense is "surrender." A central though in Islam is the peace that comes from surrendering to God. Adherents to Islam are called Muslims. (3)

Islam views itself as the final fulfillment of the biblical revelation, views Muhammad as the seal of prophecy, and regards the Qur'an as the final revelation of God. (13)

Practicing Islam

There are no churches, temples or priests, no outside authorities who determine "Islamicity"; to enter the house of Islam is to enter the mosque. Unlike a church, a mosque is an empty building, void of icons, symbols or any external religious artifacts, where the faithful assemble for prayer. Before entering a mosque, one washes hands, feet, face, ears, nose, and mouth, and is required to leave sandals and shoes outside. On Friday, the leader reads from the Qur'an and the people read silently. After the leader chants "Allah Akbar" (God is great), he and the people bow toward Mecca on hands and knees, and touch forehead and note to the rug in prayer. (13)

Key Vocabulary	***"Islam 101"*** ***These basic facts may help you in your understanding of Islam.*** ❖ *God is called "**Allah**".* ❖ ***Muhammad** is the last of 28 great prophets of Allah.* ❖ ***Islam** – means "submission"* ❖ ***Qur'an or Koran** – holy book of Islam written in Arabic* ❖ ***Mecca** – holy city, in Saudi Arabia* ❖ ***Ayatollah** – means "sign of God"* ❖ ***Jihad** – means "struggle" or "striving"* ❖ ***Infidels** – refers to those who reject Islam* ❖ ***Predestination** – the smallest detail in a person's life is decreed by God.*
Key Person or Founder, Date, Location	**Muhammad** (570?-632 A.D.) (6) Born around 570 A.D. in the city of **Mecca** in **Arabia**. Muhammad's father died before his birth. His mother died when he was six. He was raised first by his grandfather and later by his uncle. At the age of 25 he married a wealthy 40-year-old widow name Khadijah. "He was a poet rather than a theologian; a master improvisor rather than a systematic thinker. That he was in the main simple in his tastes and kindly in his disposition there can be no doubt; he was generous, resolute, genial and astute: a shrewd judge and a born leader of men. He could, however, be cruel and vindictive to his enemies; he could stoop to assassination; and he was undeniable sensual" (Anderson, 1) Muhammad had his first vision by the age of 40. At first he was unsure of the source of these visions, whether divine or demonic. His wife, Khadijah, encouraged him to believe they had come from God. Later she became his first convert. (1) About 610 A.D., in Mecca and Medina. Headquarters in Mecca, Saudi Arabia. Main sects: **Sunni, Shi'ite.** (6) ***Mohammad*** *The witness of Islam begins with the story of Muhammad (570-632 CE). Muhammad, son of Abdallah, was born about 570 CE in a Hashemite clan of the Quraysh Tribe. His father died before his birth and his mother Amina, according to orthodox teachers, heard a voice one day which told her that her son was to be a ruler and prophet, and that she should name the child Ahmad, that is Muhammad, the illustrious. He was born clean, circumcised and with the navel-cord already cut.* *The Muslim calendar dates events Anno Hegirae (A.H. – in the year of the Hijra) and begins therefore from July 16, 622 CE when Muhammad migrated from Mecca (city of his birth) to Medina where he strengthened his forces and develop a community of faithful followers. In 8 A.H. (630 CE) he. Like Joshua, led his people, the people of Allah, back to Mecca which he conquered.* *By all accounts he was said to be uneducated and poor but at the age of twelve was singled out by a Monk named Bahira who found a seal of Mohammad's prophetic office between his shoulder blades. At 25 he married Khadijah 15 years his senior. They were happily married for 25 years and although after her death he took nine additional wives he took no other wives while she lived. He had 4 daughters and two sons by his first wife but only Fatimah (daughter) had descendants who reached adulthood. Khadijah stood be him when others denounced him and it was she who*

	was the first to believe in his mission, even before he himself believed in it. (13) *At the age of 40 he began to experience dreams and visions. A lover of solitude, once a year he retired to a cave on Mount Hira where he spent a month in meditation. It was during this time that he received the first of the revelations which comprise the Qur'an. Distraught he returned and told his wife Khadijah who encouraged him to become a prophet to the people. His message of monotheism, initially taught to just his family, eventually was brought to the public.* *Pre-Islamic, Arab culture was arranged in tribal groupings and was marked by family and clan solidarity. Characteristic of the desert life was a disorganized collection of gods, heavenly bodies and demons associated with natural elements and shrines. Wealthy influential leaders in Mecca attempted to bribe Muhammad at first with the promise of wealth in exchange for withdrawal of Allah's demand that all Meccans worship the one God. But Muhammad's response was that God wanted nothing less than complete submission. For ten years, arguments, disputes, opposition and persecution were endured by Muhammad's followers eventually causing them to flee from Mecca.* *By finally, after 8 years more of skillful diplomacy and shred political maneuverings Muhammad negotiated his return. With 10,000 men, he led a march on the temporarily evacuated city on Wednesday the 10th of Ramadan in the 8th year of the Hijrah. He freely forgave the Meccans for the years of hostility he endured and granted a general amnesty to all her citizens. His army entered peaceably – no home was looted, no human indignities suffered. Going straight to the house of prayer, he purged the stone of it's 360 idols and Mecca converted to Islam.* *The prophet died in 632 CE.*
Key Writings	❖ **Qur'an (Koran),** scripture in Arabic. (6) The Koran is the authoritative scripture of Islam. About 4/5 the length of the New Testament, it is divided into 114 surahs (chapters). Parts were written by Mohammed, and the rest, based on his oral teaching, was written from memory by his disciples after Mohammed's death. (1) ❖ **Hadith** – Muhammad's words and deeds (6) Over the years a number of additional sayings of Mohammed and his early disciples were compiled. These comprise the Hadith ("tradition"), the sayings of which are called sunna ("custom"). The Hadith supplements the Koran much as the Talmud supplements the Law in Judaism. (1) ❖ **Shariah**: a combination of legal interpretations of the Qur'an and the Sunna (Hadith). Shariah means "law," and it lays down a strict and comprehensive guide of life and conduct for Muslims. It includes prohibitions against eating pork and drinking alcoholic beverages, as well as punishments for stealing, adultery, apostasy (denying Islam) and blasphemy (saying anything derogatory about Islam or Mohammed). (4) ❖ **Biblical Law of Moses, Psalms, and Gospel of Jesus (the Injil)** accepted by Qur'an, but considered by Muslims to be "corrupted". (6) These revelations include the Torah (of Moses), the Suhuf (books of the prophets), Zabur (psalms of David), Injil (gospel of Jesus). The Qur'an supercedes all other revelations and is the only one of which we still have the original text. All of the others have been corrupted, almost beyond recognition. (1)
Beliefs or Practices	*Like Christianity, Muslims accept the life of Jesus, his virgin birth, baptism, teachings, miracles and ascension but not his death upon the cross and therefore his resurrection. Muslims deny that Jesus was anything more than a human prophet. Like Moses or Muhammad, Jesus was completely human. Only Allah is divine. Islam rejects the church as the house of God while at the same time accepting the last judgment, heaven and hell and sin. With regard to the "Apostles' Creed," Orthodox Islam affirms:*

I believe in God

The Father Almighty,

Maker of heaven and earth:

And in Jesus Christ

Who was conceived by the Holy Ghost,

Born of the Virgin Mary,

Died,

He ascended into heaven

From thence He shall come

I believe in the Holy Ghost

The forgiveness of sins;

The Resurrection of the body,

And the life everlasting. (13)

Followers are called **Muslims**. (6)

Go to **mosque** for prayers, sermons, and counsel. (6)

Holy efforts to spread Islam (**jihad**). In the early part of the Middle Ages, Islam was fighting the Crusades against the Christian infidels on the basis of Muhammad's teachings on Jihad or "Holy War." Jihad means "struggle" or "strife" against something of which God disapproves. The ultimate purpose of jihad is to purify the self. Islam requires Muslims to be ready to defend the truth and to fight if necessary. (2)

Predestination: The smallest details in a person's life are decreed by God. There is freedom of choice for people, and God can change whatever he wills. Human choice and action is considered very important for everybody because we shall receive reward or punishment as a result of what we are doing. In Islam, human freedom stands in tension with God's omnipotence. (2)

Other practices include circumcision, abstention from alcohol, gambling and certain foods. (1)

Islamic Creed:

The five man articles of the Islamic creed are:

- **Belief in one God** The doctrine of predestination. The belief that no one can change what He has decreed. From this doctrine comes the most common Islamic phrase, "If it is Allah's will." (4)
- **Belief in angels** The chief angel is Gabriel, who is said to have appeared to Mohammed. There is also a fallen angel named Shaitan (from the Hebrew "Satan") as well as the followers of Shaitan, the jinns (demons). (4)
- **Belief in prophets** The Qur'an lists 28 prophets of Allah. These include Adam, Noah, Abraham, Moses, David, Jonah and Jesus. To the Muslim, the last and greatest prophet is Mohammed. (4)
- **Belief in revealed scripture** There are four: The Torah of Moses, The Psalms of David (Zabur), the Gospel of Jesus (Injil), and the Qur'an. Only the Qur'an is uncorrupted. (4)
- **Belief in a day of judgment** On the "last day," the dead will be resurrected. Allah will be the

	judge, and each person will be sent to heaven or hell. Heaven is a place of sensual pleasure Hell is for those who oppose Allah and his prophet Mohammed. (4) **Five pillars of Islam:** ❖ **Confess that Allah is the one true God and that Muhammad is his prophet. Profession of Faith=Shahada Creed=Kalima** No matter what country they live in, all Muslims share certain basic beliefs and practices. When a Muslim pronounces these words of belief, he or she formally becomes a member of the Muslim community. (12) ❖ **Pray five times daily facing Mecca. Prayer=Salat** Upon Rising, at noon, in midafternoon, after sunset, and before retiring. The worshipper must recite the prescribed prayers in Arabic while facing the K aba in Mecca. (1) ❖ **Give alms (money). Almsgiving=Zakat** Alms originally were voluntary, but all Muslims are legally required to give 1/40 of their income for the destitute. (1) ❖ **Fast during the month of Ramadan. Fasting=Siyim** Faithful Muslims fast from sunup to sundown each day during this holy month. No food, drink, smoking or sexual pleasures. The fast develops self-control, devotion to God and identity with the destitute. (1) ❖ **Make pilgrimage to Mecca (once in a lifetime). Pilgrimage=Hajj** It is expected of all Muslims at least once in their lifetimes. It can be extremely arduous on the old or infirm, so in their cases they may send someone in their places. The trip is an essential part in Muslims' gaining salvation. It involves a set of ceremonies and rituals. (1)
Who is God?	**God (Allah) is one**. God revealed the Qur'an to Muhammad through the angel Gabriel. God is a severe judge (though sometimes merciful) and is not depicted as loving. (6) There is only one true God and his name is Allah. Allah is all knowing, all-powerful and the sovereign judge. Yet Allah is not a personal God, for he is so far above man in every way that he is not personally knowable. Allah is so different that it makes it difficult to really know very much about him and unlikely that he is affected by his creatures' attitudes or actions. Although Allah is said to be loving, this aspect of his nature is almost ignored, and his supreme attribute of justice is thought to overrule love. The emphasis of the God of Islam is on judgment, not grace; on power, not mercy. (1) The essence of God is totally transcendent: God alone exits, therefore he can bring creation into being. God is eternal, no beginning and no end. God is essential – all essences derive from him. God is unique – not to be compared to anything or anyone. God's unsubstantiality: All substance is created. God's essence has no material body. God is without form. God's presence is felt everywhere. (2)
Who is Jesus?	Jesus is one of up to 124,000 prophets sent by God to various cultures. Abraham, Moses, and Muhammad are others. Jesus was born of a virgin, but is not the Son of God. Sinless. Not divine or God Himself. He was not crucified (he ascended to heaven without dying). He is referred to as messiah and **ayatollah** (ayat allah, sign of God). Jesus will return in the future to

	live and die. (6) The Muslim view of Jesus is significant. The Qur'an presents Jesus as one of the great prophets. He is called the Messiah. He is declared to have been born of the virgin Mary. He lived a sinless life (Surah 19:19). He accomplished many wonderful miracles. He is going to return to earth again to establish Islam throughout the earth. He is called "the Word of God" (3:45) and "the Spirit from God" (4:171). But they are adamant in declaring that Jesus is not the Son of God and Savior. In fact, they believe that equating anyone with God is blasphemy, the unforgivable sin. They do not believe that he was crucified. Instead, God took him to heaven without dying, and someone else died in his place. (1) Jesus is mentioned 97 times in the Qur'an, while Muhammad is mentioned only 25 times. (3)
Who is the Holy Spirit?	The Qur'an refers to Jesus as spirit of God. Muslim scholars see the angel **Gabriel** as the Holy Spirit. (6)
Human Authority here on earth	*While Sunni Muslims assume a direct relationship between believers and God, Shiites believe in the mediation of a highly trained clergy. Usually, each Shiite chooses a high-ranking clerical thinker and follows any religious ruling, or fatwa, from that person. (p.25)* (From Nine Parts of Desire)
Prayer and Worship	You cannot perform prayer if you are unclean and impure. Muslims, therefore, perform ritual cleansing. This act includes a system of ablution, which contains rich symbolic meaning. The intention of this cleansing is to purify body and soul and can be rendered invalid by deep sleep, unconsciousness, or bodily discharges. (2) Four postures in prayer are always followed: standing, bowing, prostration, or sitting. The pray-er must have clean clothes and be in a clean place, and with the right intentions towards God. (2). Gathering in a central mosque on Fridays. (2)
What about sin?	Muslims claim that humans are born with hearts that are clean slates. If they commit sins, these can be overcome by acts of the will. (4)
How are you saved?	Humans are basically good, but fallible and need guidance. The balance between good and bad deeds determines eternal destiny in paradise or hell. God's mercy may tip the balances but it is arbitrary and uncertain. (6) People have the chance to prove themselves by doing good deeds. All of us are God's managers of earth, and there is the responsibility to God to fulfill the task well. Most of us, however, choose to live in rebellion with God. (2)
What happens after death?	Resurrection of bodies. Final day of reckoning and reward. Eternal paradise for those who believe in Islam. Eternal hell for **infidels**, those who reject Islam. (6) Muslims say that Allah does not love those who do wrong, and each person must earn his or her own salvation. (4) Actions in this life will be the cause of reward or punishment in the after life. (2) Hell has seven gates with different levels and different punishments according to the measure of one's sins. (2)

Important Holy Days	**Hijrah Day (New Year):** Commemorating Muhammad's departure from Mecca to Medina and the spread of Islam. (September/October) (2) Miraj (Night of Ascent) or Lailat-al Isra (Night of the Journey): commemorating the event in Sura 17 of the Qur'an when Muhammad went with Gabriel on a winged donkey-mule from Mecca to Jerusalem where he met Abraham, Moses, and Jesus and was shown heaven and hell. (2) **Meelad ul-Nubi (The Prophet's Birthday):** Held on the twelfth day of the fourth month. The Prophet's original birthday was August 20, 510. There are processions and readings that recall the life of Muhammad. (2) **Id al-Fitr or Eid-Ul-Fitr:** Is the festival of breaking the fast at the end of Ramadan. On the first day of the tenth month of the Islamic year. People wear new clothes and visit and give presents. Charity is given to the poor. (2) **Ashura:** Held by Shi'ite Muslims on the tenth day of the first month to commemorate Husain, who was the Prophet's grandson who died in battle. For Sunnis, the celebration remembers the birth of Adam, the saving of Noah, and the Exodus of the Jews. (2) **Id al-Adha or Id al-Kabir:** The Great Festival of Sacrifice occurs during the Hajj, the Muslim pilgrimage in the twelfth month. It is the festival of the sacrifice in memory of Abraham's willingness to sacrifice his son. This is observed on the tenth day of the month of pilgrimage and is celebrated not only by the participants in the pilgrimage, but also simultaneously by those who stay in their own locations. There are prayers and a sermon, then the sacrifice of sheep, cows, or a camel. The head of each family either slays his own offering or gets a butcher to do it for him. The animal faces Mecca and is killed in one blow to the throat while the name of God is recited. The animal is then cooked and eaten and shared with the poor. (2)
Policies Towards Women/ **Gender Concepts**	The family is very important to the social economy of Islam. Marriage is required for every Muslim, even the ascetics. Muhammad commanded men to marry and propagate the race. Men may not have more than four wives, yet may cohabit with as many concubines as they choose. Although the act of marriage is important, the sanctity of the union is not as highly regarded. A Muslim may divorce his wife at any time and for any reason. On the whole, women in Islamic culture do not enjoy the status or the privileges of the men and are very dependent on their husbands. While this sounds cruel and sexist to Westerners, it is a human innovation in Muhammad's time. Islamic law requires what was then unheard of: each wife must be treated equally. Other practices include the veiling of women. (1) The Qur'an has more to say on the position of women than on any other social question. The guiding note is sounded in the words, "Women are your tillage," and the word for marriage is that used for the sexual act. The primary object of marriage is the propagation of children, and partly for this a man is allowed four wives at a time and an unlimited number of concubines. However, it is laid down that wives are to be treated with kindness and strict impartiality, if a man cannot treat all alike he should keep to one. (1) The husband pays the woman a dowry at the time of marriage, and the money or property so allotted remains her own. The husband may divorce his wife at any time, but he cannot take her back until she has remarried and been divorce d by a second husband. A woman cannot sue for divorce on any grounds, and her husband may beat her. In this matter of the status of women lies the greatest difference between the Muslim and the Christian world. (1) Since Muslim propagandists in this country persistently deny that women are inferior to men in Islam it is worthwhile to set out the facts. Surah 4:31 says: "Men have authority over women because God has made the one superior to the other and because they spend their wealth [to maintain them]. So good women are obedient, guarding the unseen [parts] because God has

<table>
<tr><td></td><td>guarded [them]. As for those whom you fear disobedience admonish them and banish them to beds apart and beat the; then if they obey you seek not occasion against them." (1)

If we approach the question of Islam's policies toward women, historically: (10)

Pre Islam	Post Islam
Marriage arrangements so loose as to be scarcely recognizable	Sanctified marriage making it the sole lawful locus of the sexual act
Women were like any other possession. (2)	
Daughters had no inheritance rights	Daughters receive half portions of the sons
Birth of a daughter regarded as a calamity, often killed	Infanticide forbidden
	Leaves open the possibility of education, suffrage and vocation
	Koran requires that a woman give her free consent before she may be wed
	Mohammad countenanced divorce only as a last resort.
	Woman provided with a sum of money which she retains in its entirety should a divorce ensue.
	Women are not the source of sin. Rather Adam and Eve are both equally to blame. (2)

Following the Bibliography is extensive information on Women in Islam from the book *Nine parts of Desire, The Hidden World of Islamic Women.*</td></tr>
<tr><td>Terminology and Definitions</td><td>Islam means "submission" (3)

Jihad – the word literally means "striving" or "struggle". In practice it is a "holy war" and can involve the promulgation of Islam by force. Many Muslims do not mind being thought of as fanatical or fundamentalist so long as they can help to achieve their stated aim – global domination. (3)</td></tr>
<tr><td>Branches/

Denominations /Number of Adherents</td><td>Islam is the fastest growing world religion. In 1900 there were 200,000,000 Muslims. In 1950 there were 370,000,000 Muslims. In 2000, there will be 1,340,000,000 Muslims. Over six million Muslims live in America. (3)

The majority of Muslims (85%) are Sunnis and a substantial minority (15%) are Shi'ites. They share the same central beliefs and practices, but differ over the issue of who can interpret the Islamic religious law. Following the death of Muhammad, disagreement arose as to the necessary qualifications and exact function of his successors as leaders (Imams) of the Muslim community.

Shi'ites: those who insist that only members of the Prophet's clan, specifically, the descendants</td></tr>
</table>

	of Muhammad's daughter Fatima and her husband 'Ali, could qualify to interpret Islamic religious law. Shi'ism has three major subdivisions as well as numerous offshoots. The majority are called Twelvers (Ithna Ashariyya), because they recognize twelve Imams beginning with 'Ali; the twelfth disappeared in 873 but will return as the Mahdi (messiah). (2) **Sunnis:** believe that successors should be appointed by community consensus. (2) **Black Muslims:** Black Muslim is a widely used name for the adherents of an American black nationalist religious movement whose self-designation changed in 1976 from "The Lost-Found Nation of Islam" to "The World Community of Islam in the West." The movement traces its beginnings to Wallace D. Fard (Wali Farad), known as "Prophet Fard," "The Great Mahdi," or "The Savior." The movement has its headquarters in Chicago, and has expanded through Fard's successor, Elijah Muhammad, who exercised strong leadership until his death in 1975. One of the best-known Black Muslim ministers during this period was Malcolm X, converted while he was in prison in 1947, who broke with the movement in March, 1964, and was assassinated 11 months later. (2)
Primary Countries	Saudi Arabia, Turkey, Yemen, Oman, Unite Arab Emirates, Qatar, Eritrea, Ethiopia, Sudan, Egypt, Jordan, Syria, Iraq, Iran, Afghanistan

Hinduism

Truth is one; wise men call it by different names. Veda (3)

Arjuna saw all the universe in its many ways and parts,
Standing as one in the body of the god of gods...
Then filled with amazement, his hair bristling on his flesh,
Arjuna bowed his head to the god, joined his hands in homage, and spoke...
I see your boundless form everywhere, the countless arms,
Bellies, mouths, and eyes; Lord of All,
I see no end, or middle or beginning to your totality.
The Eleventh Teaching
(The Vision of Krishna's Totality, Bhagavad-Gita) (2)

Key Scriptures:

God: Theistic (one God as the creator and ruler of the universe) vs. Pantheism (Pantheism "God is everything and everything is God ... the world is either identical with God or in some way a self-expression of his nature") Genesis 1:1 **In the beginning God created the heavens and the earth**

No Sin: Romans 3:23 **For everyone has sinned; we all fall short of God's glorious standard.**

No need for salvation: Romans 6:23 **For the wages of sin is death, but the free gift of God is eternal life through Christ Jesus our Lord.**

Key Person or Founder, Date, Location	No one founder. Many sects. Began 1800-1000 B.C. in India. (6) The word "Hinduism" comes from the Indus River, which flows through what is now Pakistan. (4) Hinduism is not so much a religion as a belief system. (3) Hinduism is not really one religion, but many religions that interact and blend with one another. There is no known founder of Hinduism, no creedal statements of faith to sign and no agreed-upon authority. In fact, one can be a good Hindu and believe in one god, many gods or no god at all. This is because, for Hindus, contradictory ideas are not a problem. All reality, contradictory or not, is seen as "one." (4) Hinduism is not a revealed religion in the sense of having a single founder, but evolved from the interaction between the Aryan invaders of India in thee second millennium BCE, and the indigenous inhabitants. The priests of the Aryans recited a series of hymns known collectively as the Rg Veda, and portions of this are still in use by tradition Hindus today. (5) The seven sacred cities of Hinduism are following: Varanasi (Benares), Hardwar, Ayodhya, Dwarka, Mathura, Kanchipuram (Conjeeveram), and Ujjain. Other important pilgrimage spots include Madurai, Gaya, Prayaga (Allahabad), Tirupati, and Puri. (2)
Key Writings	Many writings, including the Vedas (oldest, about 10,000 B.C.), the Upanishads, and the Bhagavad-Gita. (6)

	The Vedas: Veda means wisdom. The four Vedas consist of prayers and hymns. (3) The Bhagavad-Gita is a relatively short spiritual poem which is part of the very much longer Hindu epic, the Mahabharata. It is possibly the widest read of Hindu scriptures. (5) Upanishads: supplement the Vedas. There are over one hundred books consisting of stories, conversations and wise sayings. (3) The Great Epics: The Ramayana and the Mahabharata are the two major epic stories of India. Mahabharata includes the most popular part of the Hindu scriptures – the Bhagava Gita or the "Song of the Blessed Lord". The importance of this story is that it endorses the Hindu belief of Bhakti (devotion to a particular god) as a way of achieving salvation. The hero of the story, Arjuna, puts his devotion to Vishnu above his own personal wishes. (3)
Who is God?	God is "The Absolute," a universal spirit. Everyone is part of God (Brahman) like drops in the sea. People worship manifestations of Brahman (gods and goddesses). People are God, but are unaware of it. (6) There are 33 main deities according to the Veda. Hindus defend accusations of being pantheistic by saying that they believe that the One God has 33 different faces. (3) Hindu gods are meant to bring peace and to ward off evil spirits. (3) Among the most important Hindu gods are: Brahman, the eternal Trimutri or Three-in-One God In the Upanishads, Brahman is the name given to the One Supreme Reality, God. "Brahman" is not to be confused with the words Brahmin (the priestly caste) or Brahma (The Hindu creator-god). Brahman is beyond all description, without attributes, unmanifest, eternal, all-knowing, all-pervading, and all-powerful. (2) Brahma, the Creator is the creator aspect of Brahman, worshipped at only two of India's temples and portrayed with four heads and four arms and holding a drinking vessel, a bow, a scepter, and a book. (2) Vishnu, the Preserver The most popular is the god Vishnu, who has many names and has appeared as avatar (saviors – the incarnation of deity) in the form of a giant turtle, as Gautama Buddah, and as Rama, and Krishna, the two important heroes of Ramayana and Mahabharata. Vishnu also has many sexual consorts (wives), as does Shiva, who is worshiped by other millions of Hindus. (5) Shiva, the Destroyer (6) One of the great gods of Hinduism. He is often associated with destruction, but there are many aspects to the personality of Shiva including those of the religious ascetic and of the creator of life. Shiva can be linked to the ancient pre-Aryan fertility god of the Dravidians. Hindu worshipers of Vishnu believe that God has become incarnate many times in the past. (4) Usually portrayed as a man with a deep-blue skin, and possessing four arms with which he is supposed to be able to reach throughout the universe. Vishnu's wife is the goddess Lakshmi, who is the Goddess of Wealth. She too has four arms, in two of which shi is often shown carrying lotus flowers. (5)

Who is Jesus?	Jesus Christ is a teacher, a guru, or an avatar (an incarnation of Vishnu). He is a son of God as are others. His death does not atone for sins and he did not rise from the dead. (6)
Who is the Holy Spirit?	The Holy Spirit is not part of this belief. (6)
Human Authority here on earth	There is no known founder of Hinduism, no creedal statements of faith to sign and no agreed-upon authority. (4)
Prayer and Worship	Nearly every Hindu home has a shrine that fills a complete room or the corner of a room. (3) Hindus are encouraged to pray to images. This is meant to be a way of finding help in worship. "The Supreme Personality of Godhead said: those who fix their minds on my personal form and are always engaged in worshipping Me with great and transcendental faith are considered by me to be most perfect." Bhagavad-Gita 12.11 (3) Hindus tend to divide their acts of worship between the home and the temple, and indeed many acts of prayer and devotion take place at a shrine in the home. The shrine may consist of a shelf on which there is a statue of a god such as Krishna, and perhaps also paintings of the god in question. There may also be a lamp for burning butter or ghee, and various bright decorations. Offerings of flowers and fruit may be placed before the statue at times of worship. The temple fulfils the function of providing communal worship and may also be a focus for community activities. (5) Temples have a variety of different structures and among the Hindu community of the UK a variety of buildings have been used for temples. There is no particular structural pattern. Typically, however, a temple has an inner shrine room with the principal statue of the deity to whom the temple is dedicated. The priest will attend this deity, dressing the statue in ornate clothes and ensuring offerings of food are present. Lamps may be lit before the statue and incense burned. Leading up to the statue will be a more open area where visitors and devotees sit. Here there may also be statues of religious figures and also religious paintings. The door of the temple which leads to this large area will often face eastwards. (5) The statue of the deity may be treated rather like a human being in that early in the morning the priest may symbolically wash and dress the figure, and in the evening again wash it before the deity sleeps for the night. During the presence of the congregation the priest may well initiate an arti ceremony in which candles or lamps are lit before the deity. Prayers or readings from the Vedas take place and the lamps are then passed round the people present. (5)
What about sin?	Hindus call sin "utter illusion" because they believe all material reality is illusory. They seek deliverance from samsara, the endless cycle of death and rebirth, through union with Brahma, which is achieved through devotion, meditation, good works and self control. (4) Hindus do not think about sinfulness, which is a Judeo-Christian concept; instead Hindus are conscious of the need to perform dharma (duty). According to the law of karma, every deed, including moral deeds, binds a person to the earthly world and determines moral status. Recognized vices in Hinduism include: lust (kama), greed (krodha), delusion (moha), pride (mada), and malice (matsarya). All these vices should be avoided in thought, word, and deed. (2)

How are you saved?	Release from the cycles of reincarnation. Achieved through yoga and meditation. Can take many lifetimes. Final salvation is absorption or union with Brahman. (6) Salvation is attained through an unending cycle of birth, death and rebirth. (3) For Hindus, the great spiritual challenge is that the soul, or atman, is separated from Brahma (Ultimate Reality) and trapped in samsara, the seemingly endless process of being reincarnated over and over. Moksha, which is liberation from samsara and reunion with Brahma, is the goal. In Hinduism, there are basically three paths to moksha: the path of works (dharma), the path of knowledge (inana), and the path of passionate devotion (bhakti). (4) (See included chart illustration.) Hindus believe that salvation is to be achieved in one of the following three ways: Through knowledge, (Inana) the more difficult way to achieve moksha, which includes self-renunciation and meditation on the supreme pantheistic reality of Hinduism. This very aesthetic path is open to men only in the highest castes, and it is described in the Upanishads, a series of philosophical treatises composed beginning around 600 B.C. The Upaninshad texts teach that the world as we experience it is mere maya (illusion) and that Brahma is the only thing that really exists and has meaning. (4) Through devotion – in practice this means obeying a particular deity. (Bhakti) is the most popular way to achieve moksha. A devotee may choose any of the 330 million gods, goddesses, or demigods in the Hindu pantheon and passionately worship that particular god. In actual practic3e, almost all Hindus following the way of bhakti worship Vishnu or Shiva. (4) Through good deeds or keeping ceremonial rituals. (Dharma), a person has a set of specific social and religious obligations that must be fulfilled. He must follow his caste occupation, marry within his caste, eat or not eat certain foods and, above all, produce and raise a son who can make a sacrifice to his ancestors as well as perform other sacrificial ritual acts. (4)
What happens after death?	Reincarnation into a better status (good karma) if person has behaved well. If one has been bad, he can be reborn and pay for past sins (bad Karma) by suffering. (6) As a result of virtuous living a soul can reach a high state through rebirths. A simple way of understanding the Hindu belief in reincarnation is to think of it as "re-entering the flesh." When a person dies, he or she comes back as another person or as another animal. In this way the soul learns many lessons. Eventually it can reach a state called mukti when reincarnations cease. (3) Reincarnation is the belief that the atman, a person's uncreated and eternal soul, must repeatedly be recycled into the world in different bodies. In some forms of Hinduism, souls may be reincarnated as animals, plants or even inanimate objects. Reincarnation is the process that takes the Hindu through the great wheel of samsara, the thousands or millions of lives (all full of suffering) that each atman must endure before reaching moksha – liberation from suffering and union with infinite. (4)
Important Holy Days	There are literally thousands of different celebrations within Indian culture. At many times, similar events will be observed differently from one town to another, sand some festivals are only celebrated by certain people (often caste members) in certain areas at certain times. A few major celebrations based in Hindu belief can be found in large areas of India in one form or another. Ramanavami (Lord Rama's birthday), March/April Rathayatra (Pilgrimage of the Chariot at Jagannath), June/July

	Jhulanayatra (Swinging the Lord Krishna), July/August Raksha Bandham (Tying the Lucky Threads), July/August Krishna Janamashtami (Birthday of Krishna), August Navaratri (Festival of Nine Lights), September/October Dashara (Festival of Warriors), September/October Lakshmi-puja (Worship of the Goddess Lakshmi), September/October Dwali (Festival of Lights), October/November Mahashivratri (Night Sacred to Shiva), January/February Makara Sankranti, January Holi (Festival of Fire), February/March
Policies Towards Women/ **Gender Concepts**	Hindu women come from diverse cultural and social backgrounds, and their roles vary over time and in literary tradition. The breadth of Hindu thought and practice on this issue is impossible to cover completely, but some general points can be made: Society at the time of the Rig-Veda was patriarchal, women were given significance both in the family and in society. In particular, women's intellectual and spiritual lives were recognized, evidenced by the fact that the sacred rite of initiation marking the commencement of Vedic study was open to both men and women, and public religious rituals were performed by both husbands and wives. In time the ritual and educational roles of women became marginalized, as in the Brahmana texts where sons came to be valued more highly and rituals were enacted to prevent the birth of daughters. (2) Although a minority of learned women appear in the Upanishads (200 BCE), women ascetics are few. Hindus do not favor women taking on the monastic role. (2) The sage Dirghatamas taught that no woman should stay unmarried. A celibate woman named Kuni was told that she could not go to heaven unless she married, no personal qualities could enable going to heaven. (2) Scholars have held that Hindu myths and ideology portray an elevated view of women as both godlike and also as sexually dangerous and in need of male "taming". In some traditions of Hinduism, sexual taboos define ritual impurity. Sexual intercourse and menstruation renders one impure; a menstruating woman is treated like an untouchable. (2) In the legal texts a wife is supposed to be totally submissive to her husband. She must treat her husband as a god. Even today, a son is still preferred to a daughter, no doubt partly for economic reasons as daughters leave home to marry, while sons remain with their parents and provide security for them in old age. (2)
Terminology and Definitions	Karma – the total of an individual's acts in this life which determine his destiny in the next life on earth. (3) Karma ("action") has to do with the law of cause and effect. For the Hindu, karma means merit or demerit, which attaches to one's atman (soul) according to how one lives one's life. Karma from past lives affects a person's present life, and karma from this life will determine a person's station in the next life. (4) The Law of Karma: from good much come good and from evil must come evil. (3) Nirvana: This is the final stage where the soul arrives after it is free from all its rebirths. It is a blissful spiritual state in which the individual is freed from all desire. (3)

	Yogas: These are disciplines by means of which the body and emotions can be controlled. (3) Dharma: The Law of Moral Order, must be found and followed by each person who wishes to attain Nirvana. (3) Sanskrit: is the classical Indian language in which the religious texts of India, such as the Vedas and Upanishads, were written. Part of the interest of Sanskrit in the West is that it appears to be related to many of the main European languages: Indian and European languages have evolved from the language spoken by the tribes of the southern Asian plains in about 2000 BCE. (5)
Other Beliefs or Practices	Some disciples wear orange robes, and have shaved heads. (6) Many Hindus worship stone and wooden idols in temples. (6) Gurus demand complete obedience. (6) Disciples meditate on a word, phrase, or picture. (6) Yoga involves meditation, changing, postures, breathing exercises. (6) Foundation of New Age and Transcendental meditation. (6) The sacred cow: Hindus believe that the supreme god lives in all creatures, both humans and animals. From this they reason that all life is sacred. They think that the cow is the most sacred animal since it gives so much. In return for just eating grass and grain it gives us milk, while leather is made from its hides. (3) The caste system: Hinduism believes that the caste system, a social hierarch which governs marriages and all other major social actions, should be maintained. The four major classes within this system are: The Brahmins: the elite, linked with the priesthood. The Kshatriyas: the military class and the ruling class. The Vaisyas: the farmers and businessmen. The Sudra: the peasants. The Untouchables who are reduced to doing the most menial tasks, like burying the dead. (3)
Branches/ Denominations/ Number of Adherents	There are over 800,000,000 Hindus in the world. (3)

The Occult

There are two equal and opposite errors into which our race can fall about the devils. One is to disbelieve in their existence. The other is to believe, and to feel an unhealthy interest in them. (C.S. Lewis) (1)

---

[9] "When you enter the land the LORD your God is giving you, be very careful not to imitate the detestable customs of the nations living there. [10] For example, never sacrifice your son or daughter as a burnt offering.[a] And do not let your people practice fortune-telling, or use sorcery, or interpret omens, or engage in witchcraft, [11] or cast spells, or function as mediums or psychics, or call forth the spirits of the dead. [12] Anyone who does these things is detestable to the LORD. It is because the other nations have done these detestable things that the LORD your God will drive them out ahead of you. [13] But you must be blameless before the LORD your God. [14] The nations you are about to displace consult sorcerers and fortune-tellers, but the LORD your God forbids you to do such things."

(Deuteronomy 18:9-14 NLT)

Key Scriptures:

- **Deuteronomy 18:10-13** For example, never sacrifice your son or daughter as a burnt offering.[a] And do not let your people practice fortune-telling, or use sorcery, or interpret omens, or engage in witchcraft, [11] or cast spells, or function as mediums or psychics, or call forth the spirits of the dead. [12] Anyone who does these things is detestable to the LORD. It is because the other nations have done these detestable things that the LORD your God will drive them out ahead of you. [13] But you must be blameless before the LORD your God.
- **Galatians 5:19-21** When you follow the desires of your sinful nature, the results are very clear: sexual immorality, impurity, lustful pleasures, [20] idolatry, sorcery, hostility, quarreling, jealousy, outbursts of anger, selfish ambition, dissension, division, [21] envy, drunkenness, wild parties, and other sins like these. Let me tell you again, as I have before, that anyone living that sort of life will not inherit the Kingdom of God.
- **I Samuel 28** King Saul Consults a medium

Occult - comes from the Latin word "occultus" and it carries the idea of things hidden, secret, and mysterious. There are three distinct characteristics of the occult:

1. Deals with things secret or hidden,
2. Deals with operations or events which seem to depend on human powers that go beyond the five senses,
3. Deals with the supernatural, the presence of angelic or demonic forces.

Under the designation occult we would class at least the following items: witchcraft, magic[1], palm reading, fortune telling, Ouija boards, tarot cards, Satanism, spiritism, demons and the use of crystal balls. (1)

Necromancy - AKA spiritism or spiritualism is the oldest form of occult religion known to man. It is mentioned in the Bible as far as ancient Egypt. It is the science, philosophy, and religion of continuous life, based upon the demonstrated fact of communication, by means of mediumship, with those who live in the spirit world. Spiritualism rejects the belief in physical reincarnation, but teaches that death is a new birth into a spiritual body, without any changes in that individuality and character, and without impairment of memory. The main idea behind spiritism is that

---

[1] 11 principles of deception that fakers use to imitate supernatural or occultic phenomena (aka legerdemain): sleight of hand, psychological principles, using a stooge, unseen and unknown devices, mathematical principles, physics, physical deception, mechanical deception, optical illusion, luck and probability, a combination of all the principles. (1)

the spirits of the dead have the capacity to communicate with people here on earth through mediums, individuals who acts as intermediaries between the material world and the spirit world. This includes: séances, spirit writing, spirit raps, spirit photography, ectoplasm (mysterious substance), etc. (1)

Superstition - the belief or practice not based upon fact but upon fear or ignorance of the unknown. Including: the number 13, breaking a mirror, omens, amulets, and prayers for sneezing. (1)

Astrology - an ancient practice that assumes that the position of the stars and planets has a direct influence upon people and events. Supposedly, one's life patter can be charted by determining the position of the stars and planets at the time of one's birth.(1)

Numerology - closely allied to astrology, it is said to have its origins in the learning of the ancient Hindus. The belief holds that each heavenly body is associated with a number, which partakes of its qualities. The date of a person's birth automatically associates him with one number ... (1)

Fortune Telling - the art of forecasting the future supposedly by supernatural means. It is an ancient practice which is still popular today. Fortunetelling is also known as divination. The one who practices this activity is known as a diviner. The diviner makes use of various props to receive his supernatural knowledge, including palmistry (chiromancy), Tarot Cards (cartomancy), crystal balls and crystals (mirror mantic), and use of personal objects (psychometry). (1)

Magic - this does not include magic sleight of hand also known as legerdemain but is an attempt to master supernormal forces in order to produce visible effects. This includes White Magic (use of magical powers and abilities in an unselfish manner for the benefit of others) and Black Magic (use of magical powers and abilities to harm others).(1)

Ouija Boards - an instrument for communication with the spirits of the dead. (1)

Parapsychology - an attempt to put many of the supernatural phenomena associated with the occult on sound scientific footing such as ESP (extrasensory perception) and Uri Geller (bends items he does not touch). (1)

Satanism - the worship of Satan. Expressed in various ways: Black magic, the Black Mass, facets of the drug culture, and blood sacrifices. Traditionally, Satanism has been interpreted as the worship of evil, a religion founded upon the very principles which Christianity rejects. As such, Satanism exists only where Christianity exists, and can be understood only in the context of the Christian worldview. Things are, so to speak, reversed, and vices are turned into virtues. The Church of Satan, founded in San Francisco in 1966 by Anton Szandor La Vey has an emphasis on materialism and hedonism and Satan, to followers of this church, is more of a symbol than a reality. (1)

There are many different kinds of Satanism. The vast majority of Satanists cannot be classified as "reverse Christians" and do not accept Christian theology. Many are atheists who regard "Satan" as a symbol of individuality, autonomy, pride, rebellion, or strength. Others see Satan as a "Dark Force in Nature," or they take a modern version of Ophidian Gnosticism, which venerated the serpent of the Garden of Eden as a bringer of wisdom. (2)

Satanists are not uniform in their beliefs LaVey listed nine Satanic statements that form the Satanic "creed":

1. Indulgence instead of abstinence.
2. Vital existence instead of spiritual pipe dreams.

3. Undefiled wisdom instead of hypocritical self- deceit.
4. Kindness to those who deserve it instead of love wasted on ingrates.
5. Vengeance instead of turning the other cheek.
6. Responsibility to the responsible instead of concern for psychic vampires.
7. Man is just another animal - sometimes better, more often worse than those that walk on all fours - who, because of his "divine spiritual and intellectual development," has become the most vicious animal of all.
8. Satan represents all the so-called sins, as they all lead to physical, mental, or emotion gratification.
9. Satan has been the best friend the church has ever had, as he has kept it in business all these years. (2)

Other beliefs:

- Prayer is useless as it distracts people from useful activity.
- Heaven and hell do not exist.
- People have created gods in many forms: pick one that might be useful to you.
- Satan represents love, kindness, and respect to those who deserve it.
- Human life is held in sacred regard.
- Satan is not a being, a living entity; he is a force of nature.
- Engage in sexual activity freely.
- Practice with joy all the seven deadly Christian sins: greed, pride, envy, anger, gluttony, lust, and sloth. (2)

Paganism - AKA "neo-pagan", are people who are part of the revival of some of the beliefs and practices of pre-Christian religions. It revives the old gods and goddesses of the pre-Christian polytheistic nature religions and mystery cults such as Celtic, Norse, Greek, Egyptian, Roman, Native American religions, shamanisms, Astaroth, Diana, Osiris, Pan, Mother Goddess, and the Horned God. "Pagan" comes from the Latin words *paganus* and *pagana* meaning "country dweller" or villager. Most pagan traditions share a selection of the following:

1. A faith that was almost wiped out in the past and has since been reconstructed from ancient sources of information,
2. Celebration of main seasonal days each year, associated with the equinoxes; solstices; solar and lunar rites; and fertility, planting and harvest festivals,
3. Neo-pagans may be lone practitioners or small groups, which various traditions call covens, garths, circles, groves, hearths, etc. The largest New-pagan group is believed to be Wiccans.
4. Minimal or no hierarchical structure. (2)

Common pagan beliefs are:

1. Duotheistic or polytheistic beliefs that recognize a Goddess and God, and/or believe in many deities,
2. A pantheistic worldview; seeing deity as immanent and alive in all things, as opposed to a transcendent view of God.
3. Love for, and kinship with, Nature and the realization that all of life is a manifestation of the Divine and therefore sacred. Harming oneself, others, or nature is to be avoided.
4. Experience is more important than belief, so the emphasis is on participation and creativity in ritual and a search for the ecstatic.

5. The Pagan ethic of "Do what thou wilt, but harm none." Each individual is responsible for discovering his or her own true nature and developing it fully, in harmony with the outer world.
6. Humans are meant to have the wisdom and ability to solve their problems without the need for spiritual salvation.
7. Decentralization, with hundreds of autonomous or semiautonomous groups. Hierarchical religious organizations, self-appointed messiahs, and gurus are to be avoided. (2)

Druidry - Two reasons for the lack of information about its history and origins include the Druids' oral tradition and the colonization of their culture by the Romans. There is a vast number of theories about their history. The word Druid may derive from an Indo-European word Drus, meaning "oak" and the Indo=European wotf, meaning "to know." A Druid was literally one who "understood the oak." Other scholars think that an early Celtic prefix, dru, would suggest the meaning of druid as "extremely wise one." Modern Druids have had to study the religion of the Celts to form a picture of what Druid religion was like, but most of the information available is from biased Roman commentators such as Julius Caesar and Cicero. (2)

Wicca/Witchcraft - also known as the "Old Religion" and is an ancient practice dating back to biblical times. It is the performance of magic forbidden by God for non-biblical ends. The word witchcraft is related to the old English word wiccian, "practice of magical arts." Modern witchcraft bears little resemblance to the witchcraft of the Middle Ages. Today it embraces hundreds of beliefs and practices and has hundreds of thousands of adherents. The one common theme running through modern witchcraft is the practice and belief in things forbidden by God in the Bible as occultic. (1)

AKA "The craft. All witches are Pagans, but all Pagans are not witches. Witchcraft is closely allied to magic, but its power is often considered to be within a person or the power of a supernatural agent. Generally speaking witchcraft is human behavior that uses knowledge of and employs the world of the supernatural to achieve events that are otherwise unattainable. Many people confuse and misreport Wiccan belief. For example, many Wiccan's deviate from what was originally considered "witchcraft." They meet in covens and consider themselves witches, but they are much more in line with New Age philosophy than "traditional" (occultic) witchcraft practices. They are not Satanists; neither do they worship demons or abuse or sacrifice children, animals, or people. The major Wiccan movements present Wicca as a life-affirming, positive system of spiritual beliefs and ritual practices, although - as with any religion - certain bad practices may occur in its name. (2)

Most modern witches are followers of a nature-oriented, polytheistic faith. They believe that all life is interconnected and in the Creatress. The source of life is the Goddess, who has three aspects of Maiden, Mother, and Crone, thus representing the basic stages of life. Some witches and many neo-pagans also worship God, who may be seen as the Grain God of the harvest, the Horned God of the hunt, and the Green Man of the forest. Witchcraft shares with neo-Paganism a dislike of large organizations and holy gurus. It is mostly made up of small groups and individuals who have the freedom to disagree with their leaders. Wicca groups meet at various times and at the new and full moons for regular meetings. (2)

Wicca is part of a group of similar modern religions often lumped together under the umbrella terms of paganism or neopaganism. These groups include Asatru, Druidry, Shamanism, and Heathenism. (14)

Wiccans hold five primary beliefs:

1. The Wiccan Rede - the most important rule, this essentially states, "If it harms none, do what you will."
2. Law of Attraction - the idea that whatever one does to or for other living creatures, one draws back upon oneself.
3. Harmony and Serenity - Living in conjunction with the balanced rhythms of nature.

4. Power Through Knowledge - Learning how to tap into and control the power or energy that resides in and flows through all things.
5. Progressive Reincarnation - Learning and improving through a series of life experiences. (14)

Wicca

(AKA: witchcraft, Magick, the Craft, the Old Religion)

Key Writings	No single, official holy text (though many modern writings are widely read and respected) (14)
Purpose	To respect others, revere the earth, and reach out and within for the god/goddess. (14)
Who is God?	Belief varies person to person - adherents may be polytheistic, animalistic, pantheistic, and agnostic. Typically, God is impersonal, a creative force - both female and male - that permeates the world. (14)
Who is Jesus?	Not regarded or respected by Wiccans as God incarnate nor as the Savior of the world. (14)
Beliefs or Practices	Humans are spiritual beings connected to and part of every other spirit. (14)
Prayer and Worship	Because Wicca is an earth-based religion, the preference is for conducting services outdoors. Often these rituals are practiced by groups of witches (covens) at night. Many Wiccans opt to worship in the nude (called "skyclad"), feeling this is a more natural state and as such brings them closer to the god or goddess. These regular gatherings, called *esbats*, typically occur at the time of a new or full moon. (14)
How are you saved?	Not a rescue from sin and spiritual death, but deliverance into a magical life through practicing Wiccan beliefs and rituals. (14)
What happens after death?	Some believe in a place called Summerland; others embrace a positive form of reincarnation, eventually leading to a higher form of existence. (14)
Important Holy Days	There are eight major solar festivals (called *Sabbats)*: 1. Samhain or Halloween October 31 Festival of the dead 2. Yule December 21 Festival of the coming winter 3. Oimelic of Candlemas February 2 Heralding of Spring 4. Spring Equinox March 21 Celebration of Fertility 5. Beltane April 30 Maypole, representing the sacred marriage of the god and goddess 6. Summer Solstice June 21 Celebration of light 7. Lammas August 1 Celebration of the first harvest of wheat 8. Autumn (Fall) Equinox September 21 Feast of the ingathering (2)

Branches/ Denominations/Number of Adherents	Number of Wicca followers is difficult to determine. Some estimate: 400,000 practitioners of Wicca worldwide, 134,000 Wiccans in the US. While firm numbers are hard to come by, evidence suggests Wicca is one of the fastest growing religions today - especially among teenagers and young adults. (14)
Human Personalities Worth Noting	Margaret Murray (1863-1963 - British scholar and author of *The Witch - Cult in Western Europe* (published in 1921), which is credited for reviving modern interest in witchcraft and ancient pagan beliefs. Gerald Gardner (1884-1964) - amateur British archaeologist, who reportedly read Murray's work and then wrote *Witchcraft Today* (1954) and *The Meaning of Witchcraft* (1959), popular texts for modern Wiccans. He is regarded by many as the founder of modern Wicca. Doreen Valiente (1922-1999) - a high priestess/disciple of Gardner, who is considered by many as the "mother of modern witchcraft." The author of *An ABC of Witchcraft Past and Present and Natural Magic* (1975), Valiente continually stressed the differences between Wicca and Stanism. Silver Ravenwolf (1956-present) - leader of the Black Forest Circle and Seminary, an organization of almost forty clans (each consisting of several covens), and the author of 18 books including the controversial but popular *Teen Witch: Wicca for a New Generation.* (14)

Bibliographic Credit

Colossians map: https://theimmutableword.wordpress.com/tag/bible/

Holy Bible. New Living Translation copyright© 1996, 2004, 2007, 2013 by Tyndale House Foundation. Tyndale House Publishers Inc., Carol Stream, Illinois 60188.

The Bible Dictionary, by William W. Rand, 2013, published by Delmarva Publications, Harrington, DE

Matthew Henry's Concise Bible Commentary, Kindle Book Edition

Be Complete, By Warren Wiersbe, Victor Books, Wheaton, IL, 1984, ISBN: 0-89693-726-7

Commentary on Colossians, By Charles Spurgeon, 2014, Titus Books, Kindle Book Edition

What is prayer? By Matt Slick, https://carm.org/christianity/prayer-ministry/what-prayer

Strong's Greek and Hebrew Dictionary of the Bible, James Strong, Kindle Edition, Originally published as *A Concise Dictionary of the Words in the Hebrew Bible* and *A Concise Dictionary of the Words in the Greek New Testament*

James Hurley, pp. 82-83, citing W. Forster, ***Palestinian Judaism in New Testament Times***. London, 1964, p.124.

"Paul's Two-Year Roman Imprisonment" By Wayne Jackson, The Christian Courier, https://www.christiancourier.com/articles/144-pauls-two-year-roman-imprisonment

The Free Online Dictionary, http://www.thefreedictionary.com/

The Acts of Paul and Thecla 1:4-7, http://www.christiantimelines.com/Paul%27s%20physical%20description.htm

"Keys to Success: 6 Traits the Most Successful People have in Common", *Time*, May 15, 2014, http://time.com/99707/keys-to-success-6-traits-the-most-successful-people-have-in-common/

C.S. Lewis, ***Mere Christianity***, Copyright 1952, C.S. Lewis Pte. Ltd.

C.S. Lewis & Me, By Susan McGeown, Faith Inspired Books, Copyright 2013, ISBN 978-148-1800068

Believe & Obey, A Study in the Book of Romans about What Christians Believe, By Susan McGeown, Copyright 2013, ISBN 978-0-9835360-7-9

The Kingdom of the Cults, By Walter Martin, Bethany House Publishers, Minnesota, 2003, ISBN 978-0-7642-2821-6

Information on Gnosticism: http://www.gotquestions.org/Christian-gnosticism.html, http://www.crossroad.to/charts/gnosticism.html

Nelson's New Illustrated Bible Manners & Customs: How the People of the Bible Really Lived, By Howard F. Vos, Thomas Nelson Publishers, Nashville, 1999, ISBN: 0-7852-1194-2

Information on Colossae during New Testament Times:

http://www.theologyofwork.org/new-testament/colossians-philemon/background-on-colossae-and-the-colossians/

http://www.bibleplaces.com/colossae.htm

http://www.bible-history.com/maps/romanempire/Colossae.html

http://en.wikipedia.org/wiki/Colossae

https://www.ccel.org/bible/phillips/CPn18Philemon.htm

Bibliographic Sources for Appendix Religion Studies:

Please note: *No information in the religious studies is the direct thoughts of Sue McG unless specifically noted.*

Source 1: *Handbook of Today's Religions,* By Josh McDowell and Don Stewart, Thomas Nelson Publishers, Nashville, 1983, ISBN 0-8407-3501-4
Source 2: *A Brief Guide to Beliefs*, By Linda Edwards, Westminster John Knox Press, Louisville, 2001, ISBN: 0-64-22259-5
Source 3: *World Religions Made Easy*, By Mark Water, Hendrickson Publishers, Peabody, Massachusetts, ISBN: 1-56563-107-2
Source 4: *So What's The Difference?,* By Fritz Ridenour, Regal Books, 2001, ISBN: 0-8307-1898-2
Source 5: *101 Key Ideas About World Religions,* By Paul Oliver, Teach Yourself Books, McGraw Hill, Blacklick, Ohio, 2001
Source 6: *Christianity, Cults and Religions,* Rose Publishing, Torrance, California, 2001
Source 7: *How To Respond To Muslims*, By Ernest Hahn, Concordia Publishing House, 1995, ISBN: 0-570-04677-7
Source 8: *Know What You Believe,* Paul E. Little, Victor Books, Wheaton Illinois, 1987, ISBN: 0-89693-045-9
Source 9: *1,301 Questions and Answers About Judaism,* By David C. Gross, Hippocrene Books, New York, 1998, ISBN 0-7818-0578-3
Source 10: *The World's Religions*, By Houston Smith, Harper San Francisco, 1991, ISBN: 0-06-250811-3
Source 11: *Encyclopedia of Cults and New Religions,* By John Ankerberg and John Weldon, Harvest House Publishers, Eugene, Oregon, 1999, ISBN: 0-7369-0074-8
Source 12: *World Religions in America, An Introduction*, By Jacob Neusner, Westminster John Knox Press, Louisville, Kentucky, 2000, ISBN 0-664-25839-5
Source 13: *World Scriptures: An Introduction to Comparative Religions*, By Kenneth Kramer, Paulist Press, New York, 1986, ISBN: 0-8091-2781-4
Source 14: *The Book of Mormon* translated by Joseph Smith, Junior, Published by The Church of Jesus Christ of Latter-day Saints, Salt Lake City, Utah, USA
Source 15: *Handbook of World Religions,* By Len Woods, Barbour Publishing, Ohio, ISBN 978-1-60260-054-6

www.ingramcontent.com/pod-product-compliance
Lightning Source LLC
Chambersburg PA
CBHW081239020426
42331CB00013B/3225
9780990316848